Equity and Quality
in Digital Learning

Equity and Quality in Digital Learning

Realizing the Promise in K–12 Education

CAROLYN J. HEINRICH
JENNIFER DARLING-ADUANA
ANNALEE G. GOOD

HARVARD EDUCATION PRESS
CAMBRIDGE, MASSACHUSETTS

Paperback ISBN 978-1-68253-510-3
Library Edition ISBN 978-1-68253-521-9

Library of Congress Cataloging-in-Publication Data is on file.

Published by Harvard Education Press,
an imprint of the Harvard Education Publishing Group

Harvard Education Press
8 Story Street
Cambridge, MA 02138

Cover Design: Wilcox Design
Cover Image: Ekaterina kkch/Shutterstock

The typefaces used in this book are Sabon and Frutiger.

*We dedicate this book to
Jaime and Pilar Davila, generous
benefactors of the University
of Texas at Austin, whose substantial
gift to the university in 2014 funded
and launched our research.
Mr. and Mrs. Davila's interest in and
commitment to identifying ways
that the children most in need in
low-resource schools can benefit
through digital learning made possible
all of the work described in this book.*

Contents

Introduction

P UBLIC SCHOOLS IN THE UNITED STATES have made major investments in digital learning over the past two decades, with proponents
touting its promise for increasing equitable access to enhanced learning opportunities for all students, while simultaneously lowering costs.
Digital learning—using a digital platform such as computer, netbook,
or handheld device as an integral and consistent part of an instructional
delivery strategy—is often marketed and embraced for its potential to
offer innovative, more personalized instructional opportunities.[1] Educational technology vendors market their tools' potential to customize
content and provide teachers with real-time data on student performance
that supports the personalization of learning. It is also often argued that
students need to acquire technological skills or proficiencies to succeed
in today's labor market, and the federal government accordingly provides resources for educational technology purchases and requires states
to set aside funds for procuring technology, with the objective of closing
the "digital divide."

Equity concerns persist, however, regarding the quality of digital devices, as well as internet access and connectivity for public school students.[2] There is also a growing consensus that the thorniest challenges
schools and educators face in integrating educational technology are
not about the tools themselves but rather how digital learning interacts

1

with the systemic social, economic, racial, and historical patterns of inequity in education, or what Gloria Ladson-Billings calls the "educational debt" that has accumulated over centuries of American history.[3] In addressing the role of educational technology in promoting equity, Mark Warschauer argues that the term *digital divide* is misleading, in that it implies that investments in hardware and connectivity are key to the success of educational interventions that aim to reduce educational and social inequities with technology.[4] In 1994, only 3 percent of US classrooms had computers, while a decade later, that number had risen to 94 percent.[5] By 2019, 98 percent of classrooms had computers and 87 percent of teachers said they were using digital learning more than once per week; yet as we describe in this book, the quality of learning experiences provided through educational technology remains highly variable.[6] In fact, the question of whether equitable, high-quality digital learning is present in US schools—and what is needed to ensure that it is—has become ever more urgent. This question motivated us to partner with two large urban school districts over the past ten years to tease out the factors that facilitate or impede high-quality digital learning over time, especially in low-resource settings serving high proportions of historically disadvantaged students, where pressure to close opportunity and achievement gaps remains particularly high.[7]

The evidence and stories from the front line of digital learning contained in this book come from our in-depth study of the implementation of digital learning over time in these two diverse, low-resource school districts. The first, Dallas Independent School District (DISD), is a large, high-poverty urban school district in Texas that serves a community where 90 percent of all students are identified as economically disadvantaged. The vast majority of students in DISD are students of color with, fewer than 5 percent identifying as white, and around half are classified as English language learners (ELLs). In the second district, Milwaukee Public Schools (MPS), more than 80 percent of enrolled students receive free or reduced-price lunch, and a little over half identify as Black and more than a quarter identify as Hispanic. Wisconsin was identified in 2019 as among the most segregated states in America, with one of the widest achievement gaps in academic performance indicators between Black and white students in the nation.[8] We hence do not make any claims about the national representativeness of these school districts or the populations of students that they are engaging in digital learning. Rather, we chose these two districts because they exemplify common profiles of low-resource, urban educational settings in the US that are implementing digital learning initiatives, and also because they are not necessarily the contexts envisaged by educational technology developers and vendors when digital tools are created and marketed to the K–12 education sector. Indeed, over multiple years and across these two research sites, we have observed the "good, the bad, and the ugly" of educational technology integration.

In this book, we frequently draw on these observations as we distinguish the roles of not only technological and pedagogical factors, but also the social, economic, racial, and historical factors embedded in our education systems that influence the equity and effectiveness of digital learning initiatives. We also highlight places of promise where schools, districts, and states leverage digital tools to improve opportunities and outcomes for youth.

With the subsidization of technology purchases through the federal E-Rate program (the Schools and Libraries Program of the Universal Service Fund) and Title I funds, in combination with the eager partnership of the private sector to supply the vast K–12 market, digital learning will continue to be a growing component of compulsory public schooling.[9] Ensuring that students realize the potential benefits of digital learning, however, is a complex and often under-resourced endeavor for public schools. The evidence to date shows enormous variability in how digital learning is rolled out, accessed, and supported both during and outside of the regular school day, which harbors the potential to exacerbate rather than reduce inequities in learning opportunities.[10] In reality, the integration of digital learning into K–12 education has encountered as many missteps as it has successes, with both "high drama" failures in implementation—such as the 2013 iPad scandal in Los Angeles Unified School District—and "under the radar" disappointments (e.g., digital platforms that once held promise collecting dust on classroom shelves).[11] How schools anticipate and face these challenges has important implications for all students' learning. Stakes are particularly high in schools serving historically disadvantaged students, where inequitable access to quality educational opportunities (or the education debt) has had long-standing impacts.

About This Book

The purpose of this book is to shine light on concerns about equity in digital learning and the factors instrumental in reducing socioeconomic and racial opportunity gaps at district, school, classroom, and individual student levels in K–12 education. In Richard Milner's definition, *equity* means "providing students with what they need to succeed, regardless of their racial, ethnic, cultural or socioeconomic background," not merely equal resources.[12] A district or school with many low-income, high-need students may require more resources to implement the same digital learning initiatives equitably, rather than a comparable level of funding or personnel resources (proportionate to the number of pupils) as a more affluent district. In our research and throughout this book, we thus focus on three dimensions of digital learning initiatives that can have profound implications for how digital learning affects equity in educational opportunities and educational quality:

- *Who* in public elementary and secondary schools is directed to use digital learning tools and for what purpose (e.g., regular or supplemental education)
- *How* digital learning is implemented at school and classroom levels, including the infrastructure, environment, and supports provided to teachers and students and how it changes their role and engagement in the educational process
- *What* educational content is accessed through digital learning tools, including in blended forms (i.e., technology-assisted or -delivered instruction provided in combination with some synchronous or live instructor involvement)

Digital learning initiatives may be broad-based, with the objective of integrating digital tools into blended, core classroom instruction or supplementing classroom instruction with student-directed options for deepening and bolstering learning in creative or customized ways. At the same time, within this context of broad digital initiatives, schools and/or students also are often targeted for particular types of digital instructional opportunities to meet specific educational goals or needs. For example, DISD first introduced a districtwide, 1:1 technology pilot initiative in 2014 that sought to provide access to one laptop for each student in under-resourced K–12 classrooms. In the following year, DISD refocused the initiative on higher-poverty *elementary* schools serving larger subpopulations of ELLs and shifted to lower-cost tablets. Then in 2016, DISD refined its targeting approach again to invite school participation in the 1:1 tablet initiative based on school feeder patterns, with the goal to facilitate greater cross-school collaboration and consistent learning opportunities for students entering the same middle school in subsequent years.

MPS has likewise pursued multiple approaches to targeting and integrating digital learning in the district, while consistently prioritizing students who are falling behind in their academic progress to receive these opportunities. MPS offers online tutoring, typically outside the regular school day, for elementary school students. Students in grades 6–12 have an online instructional program that provides "data-driven differentiated instruction" in mathematics and reading to supplement regular classroom instruction. High school students are offered online courses both during and outside the school day, a program that now accounts for approximately 20 percent of all secondary course credits earned within the district. In both districts, students from low-income settings with specific educational needs—ELLs in DISD and students performing below grade average or failing courses in MPS—are given precedence for digital learning opportunities with the hope that the alternative formats, settings, and opportunities for greater personalization of content and/or pace will improve their learning and achievement trajectories and ultimately help to close racial and economic achievement gaps.

Consequently, differential access to quality learning experiences between digital and traditional classroom instruction could have profound implications for equity. For example, DISD teachers often created activity stations or group activities with tablets that allowed them to spend more intensive instructional time with smaller groups of students. In theory, this strategy would enable instructors to more effectively target and meet the needs of diverse groups of learners.[13] Depending on how it is implemented, however, this more individualized approach can also contribute to unequal access to the instructor's time and high-quality learning experiences; for example, we observed the majority of students in one classroom off-task or playing games on their tablets for most of the class period while the teacher worked with a handful of students at the front of the classroom.

There are many other ways in which the implementation of digital learning can perpetuate inequities. In MPS, for example, high school students are normally assigned to online courses after failing a course in a traditional classroom or being removed for behavioral problems or special educational needs. Given that online courses typically take place in an online learning lab rather than a regular classroom, this represents a form of *ability grouping*, in which students are segregated according to their academic performance. Research shows that ability grouping can exacerbate negative stereotypes and increase gaps between high- and low-achieving students.[14] In one stark example, MPS students traveled by bus to take online courses in a school with superior educational resources, only to be grouped in a basement classroom with a student-teacher ratio exceeding 40:1. In both this example and the DISD example above, the approach used to target or engage students in digital instruction also increased inequities in access to live instructional support.

How digital learning is implemented has implications for equity as well. Implementing a digital learning initiative in public schools is a complex and taxing endeavor, even in districts that are financially strong, with schools and teachers who are well equipped technically and supported professionally for the rollout of new digital tools, instructional models, and procedures for their administration and monitoring. Effectively carrying out the major tasks of technology integration (inside and outside of the classroom) requires the investment of valuable resources and instructional time. District staff and educators also face new challenges associated with coordinating and building capacity across district, school, classroom, and student levels of enactment and use. In low-resource educational settings—which often struggle with inadequate funding and supports and serve disproportionately high-need student populations—the typical challenges to technology integration are greatly magnified.

For example, one of the most widely acknowledged benefits of introducing digital learning in K–12 educational settings is the opportunity to deliver more personalized instruction, particularly with blended learning models that integrate substantial live interaction. Adapting the content and logistics of instruction (i.e., pace, order, location, and lesson material) for individual student needs can be especially beneficial for students with learning disabilities or those who may need additional academic support in specific content areas.[15] However, digital educational tools for personalizing and supporting learning cannot simply be deployed with same models of classroom organization and traditional instructional approaches. A review of research on instructional technologies and their effectiveness found that many school districts do not have adequate resources or supports for expanding blended learning models, and the predominant model for delivering all or most instruction in these districts offers little or no face-to-face interaction.[16] Furthermore, research finds that "drill and practice" on lower-order skills dominates the interactions of low-income and black students with digital tools.[17] Studies have also found that schools in low-income settings are more likely to experience turnover among teaching, administrative, and technology support staff, and that even when teachers in these schools have confidence in the available technology mode, they are more constrained by their environments (e.g., higher student-teacher ratios) and competing resource demands in implementing blended instruction.[18]

Accordingly, if live instruction in traditional learning settings is replaced with poorer-quality digital instruction, inequalities could be worsened, particularly for the disproportionately low-income, high-need students we see directed to digital learning. We observed many instances of digital instruction in MPS and DISD where most of the communication between students and instructors (or instructional resources) was occurring asynchronously, or where few students had access to consistent, constructive interactions with teachers and educational content in instructional spaces. In high school credit-recovery classrooms, our research and that of others find that teachers' roles are frequently confined to addressing classroom management and troubleshooting technology access issues, with limited capacity for instructional support.[19]

In addition to equity concerns about how digital learning is targeted and implemented in public schools, there also are important questions about the content accessed through digital platforms and applications, which is typically designed by private vendors for standardized delivery to the "modal student." As such, it offers few options for adapting it to local context, values, cultural norms, and the student's special needs.[20] The outsourcing of the entire curriculum and instructional delivery in online course-taking is part of a larger trend toward the privatization of education to third-party vendors, particularly for marginalized and historically underserved students.[21] This raises the question of whether the curricular content and its delivery primarily by asynchronous, online instructors creates *authentic work* for students—that is, work that allows them to solve new and interesting questions, dive deeply into a single topic, apply content to situations outside of school, and communicate ideas with others.[22] Research shows that students who are given opportunities to create their own meaning, relate course material to their own lives, and develop higher-order skills are more likely to invest greater effort and stay engaged in learning.[23]

The curricular standardization imposed by online courses is less likely to be moderated or adapted in low-resource settings through strategies such as blended learning, which are more costly to implement. For the diverse student bodies served by large urban school districts, the consequence is often online courses that do not correspond to the academic and personal realities of students' lives, which lie outside the white, middle-class norms of American society that disproportionately shape online course content. Without live instructors to adapt content to local contexts, online courses may intensify the encroachment of dominant values, norms, and expectations into schooling, potentially exacerbating the alienation of students from lower-income and minoritized populations.[24]

In sum, as districts and educators increasingly devote scarce resources and instructional time to implementing digital learning, the stakes of digital learning initiatives that overtly prioritize historically underserved student populations in large urban public schools are too high to allow educators to ignore these major equity concerns. In this book, we rigorously pursue these questions of how of digital learning changes—for better or for worse—student educational experiences and outcomes, and particularly, equity in access to quality educational content and learning opportunities. We also marshal evidence on concrete strategies that districts, schools and instructional staff can adopt to realize the promise of digital learning, even within contexts of constrained resources and high-need student populations.

Who This Book Is For

As noted above, the purpose of this book is to illuminate—with rigorous analysis of participation and outcomes, and vivid descriptions of classroom instruction—the district-, school-, classroom-, and student-level factors that support or impede the equitable and effective implementation of digital learning in K–12 public schools and describe what equity should or could look like in practice at each of these levels. It also identifies and encourages the leveraging of specific strategies and practices at these various levels that hold the most promise for reducing inequities in educational opportunities and improving student outcomes. We expect that the important lessons distilled from this work will be useful to key stakeholders of digital learning in the following ways:

- State education and local agencies and policy makers that design educational technology initiatives and purchase technology will gain a better understanding of the importance of supporting technology integration, keeping a sustained focus on implementation, and the implications for making more efficient and effective use of their limited resources toward promoting equitable student learning and outcomes.

- School leaders, district staff, and educators with responsibility for integrating educational technology to support student learning will use the information and insights to guide improvements to their own programs.

- Vendors working with education leaders and staff to enact the potential of digital tools for increasing learning will continually identify ways that they can better support educators and students in using technology and more fully realizing its potential.

- Researchers studying digital learning will learn about new opportunities for collecting and using data generated in digital learning and strengthening their methods of inquiry and analysis.

How This Book Is Organized

While some readers may enjoy reading the book from beginning to end, others may wish to read chapter 1 and then the chapter(s) most relevant to their level of expertise—district, school, classroom, or student level. Chapter 1 describes the landscape of digital learning in education and what is driving its adoption in public schools, including federal and state government funding and requirements geared toward increasing district- and school-level investments in digital learning (and reducing the digital divide); private-sector vendors that market their products to state and local educational agencies; and district- and school-level initiatives that target digital learning toward educationally and economically disadvantaged students. Within this discussion, we give particular consideration to the rationale behind targeting educational technology to low-resource settings.

The success of digital learning initiatives can be derailed in the first steps of purchasing digital tools and planning for their rollout if decisions are ill informed. Chapter 2 highlights key issues and insights for state and local educational agencies (school districts) when they first contemplate investing in digital tools, including the type of technology, the scale at which to roll it out, the infrastructure and capacity needed, and the contractual relationship with the technology vendor. This includes potential trade-offs between "high-tech" tools that may be better aligned with best practices in curriculum and instruction versus lower-cost options with differing infrastructure and capacity requirements for their integration in schools and classrooms. We also discuss the importance of bridging potentially divergent interests of the purchasing agent and vendor, planners and implementers at the district and school levels, and the users (teachers and students) in the classroom regarding expectations for technology integration and support in their implementation. Lastly, we draw on our study findings to formulate tips and guidance for states and districts in supporting the lift-off, rollout, and success of digital learning initiatives.

Chapter 3 discusses strategies for successful technology integration at the school and classroom levels. Research on school effectiveness consistently identifies the vital role of teachers in improving student learning, and technology-enhanced instruction is no exception. At the same time, the introduction of digital learning alters the integral role of the instructor—and often where instruction takes place as well—generating new instructor capacity demands and needs. This chapter extends typical discussions of professional development design and technical support delivery for teachers by focusing on the unique challenges and opportunities presented by digital learning in low-resource contexts with historically underserved student populations. We describe common instructional models and illustrate different teacher approaches to addressing recurring implementation challenges. We show how teachers' experience and beliefs about the capacity of digital tools to help meet instructional goals influence the intensity of technology use and student achievement. Lastly, we present examples demonstrating the extent to which (and how) digital learning can be adapted to meet the needs of distinct student populations and discuss opportunities for redefining the student-teacher relationship through technology to reduce inequities in student learning and outcomes.

Chapter 4 takes a closer look at who is being directed to digital learning at district and school levels, as well as how student engagement is fostered for historically marginalized students. Digital learning is an ever-expanding element of instructional programming for students, with many initiatives targeting students who are falling behind academically or at risk of not completing their secondary education. Of concern, however, are the documented disparities in how, and for what purposes, digital tools are used by students of varying racial backgrounds, socioeconomic status, and levels of academic readiness and the resulting potential for differential access to quality learning experiences that could also have profound implications for equity. Theory informs us that individuals and their social settings shape both their understanding and use of digital tools in a dynamic process through recurring interactions, and that educational technology may not always be used as intended. This chapter looks in depth at student engagement and identifies factors that limit or promote it within digital learning, as well as how those factors contribute to (or detract from) *digital citizenship*— students' actual use of digital tools compared with their intended uses. We also consider how the educational content accessed through digital tools might influence student engagement and their quality of learning experiences.

Chapter 5 highlights the potential for digital learning to be leveraged in changing students' academic trajectories. A core educational goal across state, district, school, classroom, and student levels is to use digital learning to increase student learning, achievement, and educational attainment. However, it is possible to increase attainment (e.g., of course credits or degrees) without necessarily increasing learning or achievement; and it is also possible to increase measured achievement on standardized tests without increasing learning. We take advantage of the longitudinal nature of our study to examine student educational outcomes over time and explore how access to and engagement in digital learning at different ages, grades, and in environments influences students' educational and postsecondary outcomes. We also highlight strategies for implementing digital learning that contribute to better educational outcomes and that are more (or less) effective for subgroups of students with special educational needs. Additionally, we point to student subgroups that may be left behind in terms of their educational progress and identify examples of policy and programmatic changes that could prevent these students from losing ground.

Digital learning initiatives can be effective, but it takes planning, monitoring, assessment, revamping, and refinement over time to understand and cultivate the key conditions under which they work best. In chapter 6, we summarize the concrete ways that state and local educational agencies, teachers, and others in educational settings can act on the evidence presented throughout this book to increase the effectiveness of digital learning. More specifically, we describe the levers these stakeholders have for implementing many of the strategies and promising practices that we identified for improving the implementation and outcomes of digital learning initiatives. We also describe the infrastructure we jointly created to build capacity at the district, school, and classroom levels to facilitate more productive monitoring of digital learning and retooling of approaches for its integration in various educational settings. Four key tools that we created for use by educators can be found in the appendixes included at the back of the book.

Integrating digital learning is complex and challenging work, and there is no one playbook that will work for all educational entities in increasing equity in opportunities, student learning, and educational achievement. We hope that by pointing to tools and resources for district and school leaders/staff and instructors who are looking for support in their technology integration efforts, we can collectively better ensure that digital learning access and use is equitable and promotes the ultimate goal—quality educational opportunities and outcomes for all students.

1

Contexts and Drivers of Digital Learning

I N THE INTRODUCTION, we outlined three core concerns about equity that have arisen in the implementation of digital learning in K–12 public schools. These concerns emerge despite the broader intent of digital learning initiatives to promote equitable access to new, quality-learning resources and to reduce student achievement gaps in an increasingly digitalized society and world of work. We begin this chapter by describing the digital learning initiatives and low-resource contexts where we observed their implementation. We then turn to the primary contribution of this chapter, a discussion of key drivers of increased digital learning in K–12 public schools that ultimately affect how educational technology transforms learning, for better or for worse. We distinguish drivers that are explicitly intended to reduce inequities in access to the infrastructure and tools essential to facilitating digital learning, as well as those intended to support transformative approaches to teaching and learning with technology. We also bring practical considerations of the budgetary and accountability demands that educational agencies face into this mix, as these are both drivers of digital learning initiatives as well as constraints on their implementation and efficacy in promoting equitable access and outcomes.

Low-Resource Educational Settings, Technology Initiatives, and Research Approach

The multiyear, in-depth research investigation that generated the evidence and insights we share in this book is situated in the US public K–12 educational system, where inequalities persist and create additional challenges and constraints, as well as opportunities, for the potential of technology integration to improve student learning and outcomes. More specifically, our investigation of digital learning takes place in *low-resource* settings—contexts where schools may lack sufficient funds to meet basic operating and educational costs—and where the school districts often disproportionately serve students of color, those living in poverty, ELLs, and other students with special needs. District and school leaders in these settings are typically striving to educate their students not only with inadequate funding, but also with increasing demands on those limited resources. This in turn constrains technology purchases and the infrastructure for their rollout, as well as ongoing supports for their integration and use in classrooms.

Both of our study districts, Dallas Independent School District (DISD) and Milwaukee Public Schools (MPS), received reports from their technology vendors or implementing partners (a foundation in the case of DISD) to assist in their understanding of how the technology was being used in the district and how it was affecting student performance. Such information is useful in informing district decisions about whether to continue using or expand digital learning. Ongoing evaluation can also help districts consider whether the terms of contracts with vendors are sufficient and include specifications about technology assistance, professional development, and data sharing. In partnership with these two school districts, and with financial support from external donors and foundations, we were able to expand the scope and depth of the evaluation of the districts' digital learning initiatives, including the types of student outcomes examined. On their part, district staff and teachers opened their doors and databases to the investigation and became partners in co-generating the research evidence. We also worked together to identify opportunities for the application of our findings for improving the implementation and effectiveness of digital learning in schools and classrooms.

We established our partnership infrastructure prior to start of the digital learning initiatives in each setting, which has allowed us to study the digital learning initiatives as they have rolled out and evolved. This also means that in many cases, we observed the same students over time (i.e., longitudinally) as the districts worked to implement and improve their digital learning programs. Thus, we are able to provide more than a snapshot of what these programs look like in practice and examine how the technology initiatives affected student engagement in learning and their outcomes over time.

Figure 1.1 presents an illustration of the research-practice infrastructure and activities that enabled and supported the co-generation of research evidence. The common problem of practice that we addressed was to identify the factors in implementation that impeded or supported students' access to quality digital learning opportunities and potentially reduced gaps in student outcomes. As we identified important patterns and insights, we shared this information with our district partners and used it to collaboratively identify levers for improving practice and student outcomes. In and of itself, this research-practice, continuous improvement feedback loop represents a salient, promising practice for districts in low-resource setting. In the next two sections, we describe our study districts and their technology initiatives in greater depth.

Dallas Independent School District (DISD)

As noted in the introduction, a majority of students in DISD come from low-income settings. In addition, the student population is primarily students of color with large numbers of students learning English as a second language—a population that is very different from its neighboring suburban school districts. In fact, early in our first year of collaboration with DISD, we were invited with DISD technology and teaching staff to visit a nearby suburban district to learn about its ed-tech initiatives and infrastructure. Among the most striking aspects observed during this visit were the substantial disparities in resources—from the quality

Figure 1.1

Research-practice partnership infrastructure and activities

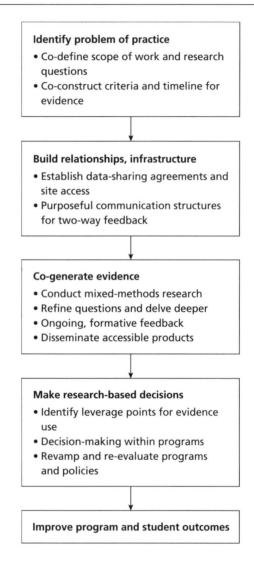

Identify problem of practice
• Co-define scope of work and research questions
• Co-construct criteria and timeline for evidence

Build relationships, infrastructure
• Establish data-sharing agreements and site access
• Purposeful communication structures for two-way feedback

Co-generate evidence
• Conduct mixed-methods research
• Refine questions and delve deeper
• Ongoing, formative feedback
• Disseminate accessible products

Make research-based decisions
• Identify leverage points for evidence use
• Decision-making within programs
• Revamp and re-evaluate programs and policies

Improve program and student outcomes

and quantity of the digital tools available for student use to the physical and instructional supports in place to integrate them into student learning. This yawning technology access gap was an important motivation for DISD's introduction of a districtwide, 1:1 technology pilot initiative in 2014. The effort got under way with teacher training sessions and the distribution of laptops or tablets to each student in under-resourced K–12 classrooms in the 2014–2015 school year. Laptops were delivered to over five thousand students in ninety-nine elementary, middle, and high school classrooms, while tablets were introduced to students in third- through fifth-grade classrooms.

In this first year of the DISD 1:1 technology pilot, we assessed student use of laptops and tablets in more than seventy classroom observations and analyses of student school records. We found that the laptops had similar rates of technical functionality and student access and that the quality of interactions between students, instructors, and the devices, as well as student and instructor engagement, were comparable to or higher with tablets versus laptops.[1] Given that the time lost to problems with technical functioning was also slightly lower with the tablets and that the average dollar cost of e-readers was about 5 percent of the cost of a laptop per student, DISD focused the majority of its efforts on tablet distribution and integration in elementary classrooms in the 2015–2016 school year.

The DISD 1:1 Tablet Initiative

The 1:1 tablet technology initiative in DISD was known as the Student eReader Program (StEP).[2] StEP was launched in conjunction with the formation of a "personalized learning partnership" that first distributed Kindle tablets to third- through fifth-grade classrooms in four low-resource schools with financial and personnel support from the Jiv Daya Foundation. Additional elementary schools were invited to the StEP program in subsequent school years, and over the course of our study, they together served a significantly higher proportion of students who were Hispanic (88 percent, or 20 percent more than non-StEP schools in DISD) and a significantly larger fraction of students with limited English proficiency (64 percent versus about 50 percent). In addition to subsidizing 75–80 percent of the cost of the tablets that were distributed to the schools, the foundation provided comprehensive training in device usage, digital resources or applications that were accessed through the devices, and training for teachers in instructional best practices. A StEP team from the foundation organized training sessions for teachers before the start of the school year and provided on-site support for managing use of the devices, troubleshooting technical problems, and guiding the integration of the tablets into classroom instruction throughout the school year. After the first year of tablet integration, schools retained access to the tablets, although they did not receive the same level of comprehensive support and professional development provided by Jiv Daya staff. Over time, the foundation developed a number of resources that were made freely available through its website. These materials included detailed guides on the basics of tablet (Kindle) use, troubleshooting technical problems (e.g., internet access, locked screens, and registration problems), managing communications via the devices and access to specific content and documents, classroom teaching tools, and subject-specific instructional resources and applications.

After receiving initial professional development, teachers chose how often and in what ways to integrate the tablets into classroom instruction. The Jiv Daya Foundation administered teacher and student surveys to the classrooms with tablets to collect information on how (and how often) the tablets were used, the types of applications accessed, and the challenges and opportunities they presented for student learning. Our research team added classroom observations and analysis of student records provided by DISD that we linked to the StEP evaluation data. Our observation instrument (see appendix A) evaluates the extent to which an instructional session (and the integration of digital tools) facilitates quality learning opportunities for students, using a set of ten indicators or dimensions of quality elements that capture the type of interactions occurring between teachers, students, and the educational technology in use, including: (1) the physical environment in which the technology is used, (2) accessibility of the technology, (3) curricular content and structure, (4) instructional model and tasks, (5) student, live instructor, and technology interactions, (6) digital citizenship, (7) student engagement, (8) instructor engagement, (9) alignment to learning objectives, and (10) how students are assessed (see appendix A). The instrument also records narrative comments and vignettes, total instructional time, and time on task; the total time a student interacts with an instructor; whether the format facilitates live interaction between instructors and students around instructional tasks; the number of students using a device; and the functionality/operability of the technology.

These data showed that, on average, DISD teachers employed some form of technology-integrated instruction for a little over an hour a day, using fully digital instructional strategies slightly more often than those that blended live instruction. We also frequently observed fluid instructional models where, for example, the classroom sessions transitioned from individual, technology-driven instruction to a teacher-led review and discussion. The following vignette from one of our classroom observations of the StEP program implementation is an exemplar of this type of fluid, teacher-led instruction:

> The students were writing a story on their tablets. When the timer went off, they turned in their assignment on tablet and also rated how they felt about their work on the assignment. The students were then immediately instructed to go to the whiteboard application on their individual tablets. The teacher had a "Kindle leader" help one student who was struggling to download the application. The teacher then projected a lesson on the screen. Students wrote responses to questions in the lesson on their whiteboard and chose a response to indicate which piece of evidence supported a particular inference. The students then shared their answers, and the teacher tallied the responses on the screen. The teacher led a discussion with the students about the correct and incorrect responses. The students then erased their whiteboards and went on to the next question. When a student figured out an easier way to clear the whiteboards on the tablets, the teacher called on that student to demonstrate its use to the class. The instructor appeared to seamlessly move students from one active use of the device to another while keeping the full attention of the students.

The above vignette exhibits several best practice lessons that we draw out of our research, including using technology to facilitate new educational experiences through active learning, interactivity, and collaboration and developing and drawing on student helpers to minimize technical disruptions and develop a sense of ownership of digital learning among students.

Milwaukee Public Schools (MPS)

MPS began implementing an online instructional program for high school students in the 2010–2011 school year, primarily for credit recovery for students who had failed a course in the prior school year, although schools differed to some extent in their instructional strategies and use of instructional and support staff in the online learning environments. The other digital tool that we studied was a free, online afterschool tutoring program in math and literacy offered to second- and third-grade students who were identified by their schools as needing additional instructional opportunities to achieve grade-level proficiency. Of those receiving free tutoring in MPS, 98 percent were identified as low-income and 80 percent as Black, and among high school students using the online instructional program, approximately 80 were identified as low-income and 70 percent as Black.

MPS Online Course-Taking

All students enrolled in online courses offered by MPS used the same vendor-provided system interface to access and complete course content. Schools typically assigned students to a physical classroom during the school day for online course-taking, where students had access to one or more instructors and devices from which to access course content. The amount of time students spent in the online classroom labs ranged from forty minutes to the entire school day, depending on the school and the number of online courses in which the student had enrolled. In the more than three hundred classroom observations conducted over the course of our study, most spaces dedicated to students completing online coursework were lab-style classrooms with rows of desktop computers on long tables or desks, although some schools utilized libraries or traditional classrooms for online course-taking.

Both MPS and the third-party vendor envisioned the implementation of the online instruction in a *blended* pedagogical approach; that is, combining both online and face-to-face instruction. The vendor's publicly available information guide on blended learning describes important roles for district staff in designing and planning a blended learning program, curriculum modification, technology infrastructure development, and "making it happen" (a role ascribed to "instructional technology staff"). The vendor-developed curriculum is delivered through asynchronous lectures, practice problems, and assessments, with lectures making up the majority of course instruction. Some courses were also designed with the expectation for project-based learning outside of the online interface, such as science labs, writing assignments, or multimedia presentations, with the vendor relying on the students' (live) assigned instructor to facilitate and grade these supplementary assignments.

Below is a composite vignette that draws on observations of online course-taking in multiple MPS classrooms and is representative of our research findings. It was created to illustrate the instructional setting and interactions of a typical computer lab reserved for students enrolled in online courses.

There are thirty computers in the large lab-style classroom. All students sit at their desktop computers, working on various course modules that depend on where they need to recover credit. Twelve of the fifteen students are wearing headphones and are plugged into the computer. Students are talking quietly, occasionally laughing. Ten minutes into the class period, the teacher stands up and walks around to check on the students, at which point nine of the fifteen students are actively working in the online course system. The teacher emphasizes that the students need to strive for the goal of completing 3 percent of their coursework per week. He tells them to focus more and to take advantage of the resources they have both during and after the school day. The students are a distraction to each other, with some students walking around and disturbing others or talking out loud. There is no redirection of students on the part of the teacher. Toward the end of the period, five of the students are still actively clicking, looking up at the screen, typing, etc. Two of these students also have a paper notebook out. These students are engaged in an iterative process of reading content off the screen and then writing it down in their notebooks. One student is toggling between the online course program and Google to look up terms. At any one time, four to five students are checking their phones, and one or more are sleeping.

As we frequently observed, the instructor in this vignette interacted with students in a predominately motivational versus instructional role, with few students accessing instructional content consistently throughout the class period.

MPS Online Tutoring Initiative

MPS's online tutoring program (provided by another external vendor) was made available in twenty-two different schools to second- and third-grade students who were economically disadvantaged and performing below grade level. MPS established a research-based program goal of serving each student with at least forty hours of tutoring in the school year, with no more than two to three hours of tutoring per week.[3] The expected tutor-to-student ratio was 1:2, although some tutoring sessions provided 1:1 tutoring (as requested by the parent). There was no set schedule for student tutoring or tutor rotation; students could schedule their tutoring sessions at their convenience. In general, tutors were assigned to work with a particular group of students, but this could also fluctuate depending on scheduling needs. In the tutoring sessions, students logged onto the online tutoring system using a computer either at home or at school, where they interacted synchronously with a remote instructor. Students interacted individually with the teacher or in pairs, allowing for more targeted attention than feasible in a traditional classroom setting.

Data from the vendor tutoring records showed that the large majority of participating students received forty or close to forty hours of tutoring in this program. The program allowed students to interact with a teacher as they would in a typical classroom setting, but with more targeted attention that was facilitated by allotting only one or two students per tutor. The modifications and accommodations made by tutors for their students tended to include readability of text, pacing and flexibility, creating incentives (e.g., playing a game at the end of the session), and individualized assessments both via the technology and instructors. At the most basic level, tutors individually graded and provided feedback to students, which in turn supported teachers in targeting individual student needs for assistance. For instance, in one observation of an online tutoring session involving two students, the students started the lesson by writing a complete sentence about their day, identifying and reading definitions of abstract and common nouns, and then reading sentences and putting the correct missing word in the sentence. The tutor adapted instruction by activating prior knowledge, asking questions, providing context clues, and other opportunities for each student to demonstrate learning. However, technical difficulties occurred frequently, and with a few exceptions, the tutors struggled to understand and troubleshoot them. These technical disruptions appeared to affect both the quantity of instructional time provided to students and the quality of the interactions between the student and the instructor and/or technology.

We now turn to a discussion of the broader drivers of digital learning—beyond the (micro) district and school levels described above—beginning with how recent public investments in telecommunications infrastructure and connectivity have progressively made a difference in students' access to digital learning opportunities in the classroom.

Drivers of Digital Learning

Infrastructure Investment and Digital Development

It was not long ago that the distinctive screech of a dial-up modem signaled our connection to the internet. While computers first brought digital learning to classrooms in the 1980s, as of the end of the 2000, only 7 percent of internet users in the United States benefited from the faster and more reliable connectivity facilitated by cable or DSL broadband service.[4] Government policies subsidizing broadband access and simultaneously promoting privatization and competition in the telecommunications industry have been credited with expanding the quality, availability, and affordability of the internet and broader access to digital resources.[5] The federal E-Rate program was first established through the Telecommunications Act of 1996, which sought to bring about universal access to affordable telecommunications services with funding garnered through mandatory contributions from telecom providers. Importantly for K–12 public education, the Act required companies to provide telecommunications services to public schools and libraries at discounted rates from 20 to 90 percent off, depending on need (determined by the fraction of students receiving free and reduced-price lunch) and the type of service. In addition, other funds supporting foundational investments in educational technology were earmarked in less obvious places throughout the US Department of Education budget.[6]

As the unit prices of hardware declined and made purchases of educational technology for large-scale distribution more affordable, concerns about a digital divide shifted to the quality of internet access and connectivity for public school students.[7] In a 2014 modernization plan, the Federal Communications Commission (FCC) narrowed the focus of the E-Rate program to increasing affordable access to high-speed broadband and boosting access and the bandwidth of Wi-Fi networks in public schools. By the end of 2016, approximately 77 percent of school districts were meeting the minimum federal connectivity targets of internet speeds (100 megabits per second [Mbps] per one thousand users), compared with 30 percent of school districts in 2013, at less than a third of the cost per Mbps.[8] And in 2019, 99 percent of schools were benefiting from the faster fiber optic connections. As a matter of fact, over the course of our study, we saw firsthand the difference that improved internet connectivity made in accessing and realizing the capabilities of digital learning tools in the classroom. Faster and more consistent internet service opens opportunities for teachers to integrate the use of online educational applications and other software into classroom instruction that are not pre-installed on devices, and it also reduces disruptions to learning associated with technological difficulties, slow internet access, or disconnection.

Consider, for instance, this example from one of our earlier (2014–2015 school year) observations of 1:1 laptop use in DISD: A teacher intended his ninth-grade biology class to use the internet to understand a system for classifying and naming organisms. However, although pairs of students attempted to connect to the internet via their Lenovo laptops, they were unable to gain any consistent internet connectivity for the first thirty minutes of class. This failed connectivity forced the students off the technology, and the instructor had to redirect students to a traditional, hard-copy instructional format, which made the lesson less adaptable/customizable for individual student learning needs. Students also lost instructional time as the instructor spent a large share of the class period attempting to help the students access the planned lesson before giving in to the hard-copy alternative. In the high school classrooms in MPS where students were accessing their courses online, slow internet access contributed to delays in loading course content, which slowed student progress and discouraged their engagement; on rarer occasions, internet connectivity was lost entirely and brought all course activity to a halt. However, over time, and across all digital tools and contexts, we recorded fewer and fewer digital learning sessions in which time was lost to such technical issues; and by the 2017–2018 school year, fewer than 1.5 percent of our observed sessions of digital learning documented instructional time lost to technical issues (compared with 32 percent in the prior two years).

Clearly, public investments in improving basic infrastructure like internet access increase the potential for digital learning to be more effectively deployed in public schools, but these investments will need to continue to keep pace with continually evolving technologies that aim to increase personalized and adaptive learning. The coming wave of digital learning tools in education is expected to require infrastructure capable of supporting multiple technologies on-site and in the cloud and massive data storage and transport, along with hybrid cloud and network environments, high-speed broadband, and other networking components.[9] In fact, beginning in 2018, the FCC raised the minimum recommended bandwidth to enable digital learning in the classroom to 1 Mbps (from

100 kbps) per student. This environment will also require more skilled personnel in IT support, as well as classroom teachers with advanced technology training—often a scarce resource in large, urban school districts. In our interviews with school district staff and instructors, we regularly heard about the lack of on-site (school-based) IT support and the limited training provided by vendors of digital tools for unleashing their capacities in the classroom. When an IT staff member in DISD was asked about resources in the IT budget for expanding technical support at the school level, he starkly remarked that their technology budget could barely cover the cost of replacing light bulbs for the overhead projectors.

Private-Sector Penetration

The private vendors developing and marketing educational technology to public schools have not only benefited from the public investments in infrastructure and subsidies for technology purchases discussed above, but also from legislation such as the No Child Left Behind Act of 2002 that sought to increase the role of market-based mechanisms in improving educational opportunities and choice for children, particularly those in low-performing public schools. NCLB followed on the worldwide wave of New Public Management (NPM) reforms of the 1990s that encouraged the devolution of government functions and managerial responsibilities to the private sector to promote a more efficient, competitive, and results-oriented public sector. The push under NCLB for more private-sector involvement to promote "flexibility, choice and accountability for results" led to the embracing of a growing, more institutionalized role for private actors and big business in public education, including, for example, in home schooling, charter schools, and the instructional core of traditional schools as well as in supplemental educational services.[10] Under NCLB, public schools that were not making adequate yearly progress in increasing student academic achievement for three consecutive years were required to offer parents of children in low-income families the opportunity to receive extra academic assistance (or to transfer to another public school), drawing on the private sector to offer eligible students a range of choices. The requirement to rely on private providers to deliver these supplemental educational services opened a new multibillion-dollar (annual) market for vendors. Education technology companies moved in to offer these services using digital tools, and private-sector investment in K–12 digital education tripled over this period, as big ed-tech vendors came not only to dominate supplemental educational service provision in many of the largest school districts, but also to expand their role in regular classroom instruction in schools.[11]

In their book *Equal Scrutiny*, Patricia Burch and Annalee Good described this "storm surge" in digital education as linked with a national policy agenda under the Obama administration that included the Race to the Top initiative, the adoption of Common Core State Standards, and the corresponding authorization and streamlining of large-scale contracts with corporate education technology partners (Apple, Cisco Systems, Pearson, and others) to purchase educational technology and digital instructional tools to "transform instruction, curriculum and assessment at every level of schooling."[12] These federal drivers of digital instruction were reinforced by state and local efforts that invited private vendors to become partners in the integration of educational technology into K–12 public education, such as the Shared Learning Collaborative formed under the leadership of the Council of Chief State School Officers that brought together state and district educational leaders, teachers, foundations, and big ed-tech vendors to collaborate in using technology to improve educational outcomes. Nearly all states now require some form of digital education as a learning option for public school students, and some states and districts also require completion of an online course as a condition of graduation.[13] These efforts are motivated in part by the argument that students need to acquire digital learning competencies to succeed into today's labor market and duly fueled by concerns about a growing digital skills shortage across industries. Researchers studying the "digital skills divide," however, distinguish it from the "internet access divide" and caution that simply ensuring access to the internet and educational technology will not mechanically confer the benefits of learning with technology and the skills students need to be competitive in the labor market.[14]

Push for Personalized Learning

Advances in digital tools, computational power, memory storage, and internet connectivity continue to encourage new visions of how technology can transform learning for public school students in ways that support higher-order thinking skills and individual students' learning needs. The Every Student Succeeds Act (ESSA), enacted in 2015, provides for the use of federal funding by state and local educational agencies to support a *personalized learning* approach; that is, one that tailors learning to students' individual needs and interests and allows them choice and flexibility in how mastery of standards is attained. Even more explicitly, ESSA requires school districts receiving $30,000 or more in funding to assess student needs for "access to personalized learning experiences supported by technology and professional development for effective use of data and technology."[15] In addition, requirements for implementing personalized learning approaches have been adopted by at least three states, while other states are currently laying the groundwork for more systematic implementation of personalized learning.

Within this broader conceptualization of personalized learning, Noel Enyedy distinguishes opportunities for personalizing *instruction*—"tailoring the pace, order, location, and content of a lesson" for an individual student—from personalization of the *learning process and environment* through new ways of teaching and integrating digital resources to effectively engage students.[16] We have seen teachers strive to and skillfully deploy digital tools to personalize both instruction and the learning process for students, consistent with their own teaching goals and philosophies or aspirations for their students.[17] At the same time, we have observed and heard about the many constraints they face to fully and regularly realizing the potential of digital platforms to support personalization.

For example, one MPS teacher we interviewed was taking courses online with his students so that he could not only help them adjust the pace of instruction and better support their content learning, but so that he could also develop appropriate supplemental instructional materials that he used in a blended learning approach to deepen students' learning of the course content. This same teacher, however, described a long list of frustrations with his efforts to provide personalized and blended learning opportunities for students with technology, including high student-teacher ratios and inadequate time for one-to-one interactions in the classroom; administrative pressures to move students faster through their online courses; and limitations of the physical environment (including a lack of resources for ensuring the physical security and operability of 1:1 devices). The impetus for students to accumulate credits more quickly appears to be driven in part by the hierarchical chains of school performance accountability, with principals similarly reporting pressures to ensure that high school students graduate within the expected four years, regardless of whether the student performance data suggests that they require additional time for content mastery.[18]

The push for personalization of learning is nonetheless a major part of "big business" in K–12 education, with some of the same companies that are developing the software and digital tools for tailoring instruction also supporting their adoption and implementation by school districts—and sometimes their evaluation as well.[19] In fact, one of the most comprehensive studies of the implementation and effects of personalized learning to date, conducted by RAND, has been funded by the Gates Foundation, and it does not minimize the challenges or downsides of digital personalization efforts. Moreover, the same research report that documents some of the national factors driving personalized learning, also supported by the Gates Foundation, finds that when one digs deeper to examine what is happening in schools and classrooms, "most are only dipping their toe into personalized learning."[20] The study documented that only about a fifth of elementary and middle schools indicate capabilities for personalizing instruction (e.g., the pace at which students proceed through content), and there was little evidence that the learning processes and environments were being substantially transformed through personalization efforts. This was also true for high schools, where teaching loads tend to be greater and it was more challenging for teachers to get to know the individual students' strengths and needs. Moreover, another recent RAND report was forthright about teachers' concerns about the quality of students' learning experiences in online programs, in part because of the perceived low quality of the curricula offered by the vendor, but also because teachers acknowledged their heavy reliance on the online program to adapt the pace and content of instruction for students.[21]

Budget Pressures and Accountability Demands

If education technology vendors design their products with blended learning models and personalization strategies in mind for their implementation in the classroom, one might question why schools are not doing better at implementing digital learning in these potentially transformative ways. The director of Digital Learning Initiatives at the Dartmouth Center for the Advancement of Learning explained that schools and educational technology vendors believe that digital tools, "when properly utilized," can be "leveraged to expand educational access and increase quality."[22] However, implementing blended and personalized learning well cannot be done on the cheap. It requires more inputs in the form of instructor time, the development of materials to aid in the redesign of courses, coaching and other instructional supports in the classroom, and readily available IT support just to get started. In addition, although digital learning tools typically include clever features for capturing data that can be invaluable for teachers in differentiating instruction and guiding student learning with them, many teachers need extensive and ongoing training and support to exploit those capacities. A RAND Education study of high school personalized learning initiatives found that teachers and principals in nine out of ten schools did not have sufficient time, resources, or training to develop the materials, strategies, or supports for implementing quality differentiated instruction, with teachers lacking capacity for even customizing the pace of learning for their students.

Given these persistent time and resource constraints, we have frequently observed instructors employing strategies for technology integration that effectively ration their time with students in blended or personalized learning endeavors. Take, for example, this observation of students working with 1:1 laptops in stations in a DISD grade 4 classroom:

Throughout the class period, the instructor worked with a small group of six students on mathematics problems. The other students in the classroom were directed to work on "STAAR readiness exercises" on their laptops; that is, self-directed practice on problems of simple addition and subtraction, calculating perimeter of shapes, etc., in preparation for state standardized tests. The students appeared to move (slowly) through the questions like worksheets, and in the absence of attention from the classroom instructor, they were constantly distracting each other from their work on the computers. The instructor only engaged with these students for disciplinary purposes or to call for a change of stations. When after several rotations, the students were no longer working on their laptops, the instructor required all students to shift back to desk work (i.e., worksheets).

The RAND Education study also found that teacher incentives to adapt the pace of digital instruction to students' individual educational needs were diminished (rather than bolstered) by pressures to prepare students for high-stakes assessments. Indeed, across schools (and grade levels), we frequently saw teachers turn to digital tools to facilitate student preparation for end-of-year state accountability tests, but often with limited instructor guidance for personalizing *instruction*, and no meaningful personalization of the *learning process*. For instance, we observed multiple instances in Dallas elementary classrooms where students were directed to complete an "exit test"—a written math problem that they turned into the instructor following their self-directed digital test practice—before they could leave the class.

At the high school level, we were more likely to observe teachers focusing their limited time and efforts on blending or personalizing instruction for students who they believed were more interested in learning with digital tools. In one example, the teacher explained in a post-observation interview that she was trying to help the students in the class who wanted to make progress. She shared her log of how she tracked student progress toward online course completion; of more than thirty students on the roster, few were progressing, and many were not attending school at all. On the day of our observation, only ten students were in the classroom at some time during the period, and the teacher worked individually with only two of them. A student yelled to the teacher that he did not have access, but nothing happened. There was a lot of coming and going from the classroom, but ultimately, about eight students stayed for most of the period. Four had Chromebooks out, but only one or two were working on a course at any given time.

In contrast, we observed more consistent instructional assistance in a high school classroom where students appeared to be working (and taking notes) throughout the observation. In a classroom with two teachers, one of the teachers walked over to a student writing out an assessment problem on a whiteboard and asked what she was doing. The student said she needed help. The teacher drew the problem on the whiteboard, then went directly into the student's notebook to find the materials with which she could solve the problem The teacher had her try, then they spent eight minutes going directly back and forth around the problem, both writing and drawing on the whiteboard, "Where do these triangles overlap?" The second teacher came in and checked in with this same student before giving her a worksheet to reinforce her understanding of the Pythagorean theorem. Then the second teacher went to a different student with a question. She brought over a whiteboard and markers, and she and the student used that to talk through specific problems together and then respond on the screen via student's desktop. The teacher encouraged the student, "Okay, now you have to write this in your notebook." They wrote some notes and explored the problem again. The teacher prompted, "Where is the Y intercept?" and the student pointed. The teacher then encouraged the student to continue working through the problem using her notes for reference.

In *Rac(e)ing to Class*, Richard Milner points out that the "locus of control" and burdens for transforming learning opportunities for children are typically placed on individual teachers. In the online course-taking settings we observed, modifying or individualizing the standardized course structure typically required facilitation by a live instructor. In the example of the MPS high school classroom, with more than two-thirds of the students absent from class, the teacher was not constrained by a high student-teacher ratio from interacting one-to-one with more students in the classroom, yet the allocation of instructor time and attention across the students was clearly inequitable. Our classroom observation data revealed that instructors were more likely to provide intensive, learning-focused assistance to students who requested help, although as in that particular example, we also observed students failing to gain teacher attention, especially if they were less assertive in their requests. We found that teachers who took the time to build rapport with their students by demonstrating an interest in their lives outside of school (as well as their needs in the classroom) were more successful in engaging and supporting students in their learning, particularly those that Milner generally describes as "school-dependent" (i.e., students who not only rely on schools for their academic nurturing, but also their "social, emotional, behavioral and affective development").[23]

These observations and insights from our analysis raise an important policy question that will continue to arise as the use of digital learning expands: If we expect instructors to be prepared to fill highly skilled, blended instructional roles as well as non-instructional roles—such as counselor or confidant—in personalizing learning with digital tools, are state and local educational agencies prepared to invest more in the inputs required for their successful (and equitable) rollout and integration in schools? This will require, as Milner calls for, additional, higher-level and systemwide efforts—including more tailored professional development and reduced administrative demands—to support teachers in transforming both the learning process *and* teacher roles in the classroom in ways that reach "every child in every classroom."[24]

Launching Digital
Learning Initiatives

THE KEY DRIVERS BEHIND THE UPSURGE in online learning in US
public schools—dynamics related to infrastructure, privatization in
K–12 education, tech-heavy reform models like personalized learning,
and budgets—are prevalent not only on the national level, as discussed
in chapter 1, but also are expressed in state and district level contexts.
This chapter primarily focuses on the ways in which district-level factors and decisions influence the rollout of digital learning initiatives, beginning with how states facilitate or constrain decisions and conditions
in the districts. We start by showing briefly how elements of the state
policy context and education systems in both Wisconsin and Texas, reflect some of the broader drivers of digital learning initiatives and affect
the level and types of resources available locally for implementing them.

The Wisconsin and Texas Contexts for Digital Learning

State-level policies on digital learning are designed to encourage and
support school districts and schools in launching and sustaining digital
learning initiatives. In 2012, the Digital Learning and Technology Team

at the Wisconsin Department of Public Instruction (DPI) put into place the Wisconsin Digital Learning Plan, which provides districts with tools and guides aligned to the Future Ready Framework.[1] The framework focuses planning and implementation of personalized digital learning on seven "gears" that align with many of the factors critical to the successful roll out of digital learning, including: curriculum, instruction, and assessment; personalized professional learning; robust infrastructure; budget and resources; community partnerships; data and privacy; and use of space and time.

The Wisconsin Digital Learning Plan includes the Wisconsin Digital Learning Collaborative (WDLC), which describes its mission as "to provide equitable access to high-quality online education by offering online learning to school districts, cooperative educational service agencies, charter schools and private schools located in this state."[2] The WDLC consists of two collaborating organizations: (1) the Wisconsin Virtual School (an organization providing online courses and support) and (2) the Wisconsin eSchool Network. Personalized learning has been adopted by a number of school districts and schools, and the state is home to the Personalized Learning Institute, run by one of the eleven Cooperative Education Service Agencies that support professional development and implementation. Wisconsin adopted the most recent version of the Wisconsin Standards for Information and Technology Literacy in 2017.

Although the state does not require students to take an online learning course for high school graduation, some districts have implemented their own criteria. For example, Milwaukee Public Schools (MPS) requires students to complete either an online learning course, community service experience, or service-learning course. Despite the steady cuts to state appropriations for K–12 education between 2010–2018, a number of grant programs are still available for districts, offered through the state and supported by both public and private funding. They cover areas such as digital curriculum development and STEM instruction, as well as both teacher training and infrastructure grants targeting rural districts. Recognizing the importance of connectivity, the state also has "BadgerNet," a public-sector telecommunications network that brings additional capacity to schools at a fraction of the cost charged by commercial suppliers.

Over the past ten years, Wisconsin has also put a number of policies into place that facilitate privatization within the K–12 education market. Policies related to voucher school expansion have made additional public funds available to virtual schools run by either private entities or by public districts that purchase digital course-management systems and software. As of the 2017–2018 school year there were forty-two online or virtual charter schools in Wisconsin, serving over seventy-five hundred students, approximately six hundred of whom were MPS students.[3]

We see many of these same dynamics at work in Texas. The Texas Education Agency (TEA) established a Long Range Plan for Technology in 2006. The plan includes the Classroom Connectivity Initiative, which leverages federal e-Rate funds with approximately $25 million in matching state funds to support districts in improving their infrastructure bandwidth and school-level wireless internet capacity.[4] For sixteen years, TEA partnered with the Regional Comprehensive Center to host the "ePlan" system where districts would submit technology plans. (The ePlan was discontinued due to lack of use in June of 2019.)

The Texas Essential Knowledge and Skills (state standards), which aim to align curricula across the state, include Technology Applications in elementary, middle, and high school; these specify expectations of students related to their understanding of "technology concepts, systems, and terminology." Although neither the state of Texas nor Dallas Independent School District (DISD) require completion of an online course for high school graduation, state policy does mandate that: "Each school district or open-enrollment charter school shall adopt a written policy that provides students with the opportunity to enroll in electronic courses provided through the state virtual school network."[5] TEA also runs the Texas Virtual School Network, which draws on public funding to provide free supplemental accelerated coursework (e.g., AP courses, dual enrollment), online foundations courses (e.g., language, career, and technical education), and six full-time online virtual schools serving grades 3–12. In addition to the schools in this network, as of the 2016–2017 school year, there were ten full-time virtual charter schools in Texas, serving around ten thousand students.

As the above discussion suggests, states leverage key financial and administrative resources for districts and schools that are critical to strengthening local technical and organizational capacities for rolling out digital learning initiatives. Yet it is at the district level, as we discuss below, "where the rubber meets the road" in determining whether the goals of equity and quality in digital learning are realized in K–12 public schools.

How Factors at Rollout Influence Long-Term Costs, Implementation, and Outcomes of Digital Tools

Several district-level factors influence the implementation of digital tools in classrooms. Some are critical to the improvement of the integration efforts, while others are barriers. We see these salient factors as falling into one of two categories: capacity or processes.

District Capacity

Across the US, district decisions regarding technology initiatives typically have baked-in assumptions—often unfounded—about elements and capacities at the school level that are critical to digital learning. These include assumptions about the quality of internet connectivity and hardware to support initiatives; teachers' access to tech support; the knowledge and skills of teachers implementing the initiatives, and the frequency and nature of professional development provided by the district. We address each in turn.

Connectivity and Hardware

In the classrooms we observed, most students had full access to devices and the digital instructional environment with minimal interruptions from technical problems. In fact, we saw a decrease over time in the amount of instructional time lost to technical issues. This decrease coincided with investments on the part of the districts in digital infrastructure at the school and district level (in addition to the federal efforts described in chapter 1) to improve internet capacity. That said, it was clear that both the districts and vendors of digital tools had particular expectations for the quality of both internet connectivity and the hardware of digital learning that was not always met in practice.

First, many digital learning tools are dependent on the internet and assume full connectivity for instruction to happen. Yet in the districts we observed, district- or school-level internet capacity issues could slow, or in the case of outages, completely halt the effectiveness of these tools for instruction. For example, when Wi-Fi is not at full capacity, video lectures load slowly and students lose instructional time while waiting. Milwaukee Public Schools' online tutoring program provides examples of the difficult interplay between connectivity issues and the functionality of the software itself. In one lesson, typing was slow to appear on the screen, and some of the sentences appeared in a vertical column instead of a horizontal row, which made it challenging for the teacher to read and provide feedback. In another session, a student described Martin Luther King, Jr.'s "I Have a Dream" speech audio as sounding like King was talking in a tunnel. In both instances, infrastructure limitations slowed and lessened the effectiveness of educational opportunities. The challenges of implemented digital learning outside of the school day might be even more severe, as students in lower-income districts often do not have sufficient infrastructure to support these programs at home.

In addition to connectivity, districts and vendors count on classrooms being equipped with enough hardware (desktop computers, Chromebooks, tablets, etc.) for students to readily access the programs. They also assume that the hardware is consistently in working condition, usable by the students it is intended to serve, and sufficiently up-to-date to be able to support the technology. For example, in one classroom, text on the (tablet) screen was extremely small, so several (students) had to hold up their Kindle and bring it close to their face, while others hunched over to get closer to the screen. Furthermore, there seems to be a disconnect between district notions about what supporting hardware is available (e.g., locks for Chromebooks, headphones, projectors) and the class-room-level reality. For instance, very few of the credit-recovery class-rooms we observed universally provided headphones to students. When they did, it was typically because the instructor had purchased them with personal funds. One teacher reported spending about $130 per year buying earbuds for students. Other students brought their own headphones or listened at a very low volume through the computer speakers.

Not only are the assumptions districts make about internet connectivity and hardware important independently, but they also relate to one another. For example, in one observation, we noted that technology issues in reality took over the majority of the lesson. Between long transition and instructional periods and YouTube access issues, students received only seventeen minutes of instruction. The issue was not internet connection–related, but rather the settings on the Kindle for accessing YouTube videos. This occurred even though the instructor had tested YouTube access to the videos in another class and the device had worked properly. Also due to tech issues, students were not all using individual devices to access YouTube videos, requiring some to share the small screens to view the content.

In another example, the purchase of carts of Chromebooks to increase access to digital learning opportunities actually had the opposite result when the increased use of Chromebooks overloaded the existing Wi-Fi capacity of the school and slowed accessibility.

Technical Support at the School Level

It is common for low-resource districts and schools to have limited staff dedicated to tech support. Some vendors of digital tools offer live tech support via phone or web-based chats that teachers can access. Our study districts also had district-level support that teachers could call, but often these issues could not be resolved by district or vendor support within a class period. Therefore, the burden of addressing the tech issues shifted to the teachers (and sometimes students) in the classroom. Tech support often came down to teachers attempting to address these issues on their own in real time. Classroom teachers thus had to make rapid, on-the-ground pivots in planning and implementation of their lessons to cope with problems in accessing digital educational content and to salvage instructional time for their students.

Classroom Teacher Capacity and Professional Development

Along with the knowledge and skills that classroom teachers need to have in traditional classroom settings (curriculum planning, instruction, assessment, classroom management, etc.), the integration of digital tools requires specific capacities of the adults charged with facilitating student learning. The use of digital tools increases technical demands on teachers and may also increase the need for, or challenges experienced in, classroom management. In addition, high-quality learning with digital tools is not possible in any educational setting without effective instructional strategies. Comfort, adaptability, and flexibility are essential to integrating technology in a manner that enhances rather than subverts strong instructional practices. It is also important to note that student learning be can affected by the capacity of other adults in the instructional space, such as the parents' capability to support their children in online, home-based tutoring or the availability of bilingual resource specialists to support English language learners in school.

We've observed three particular areas in which assumptions at the district level about teacher capacity became critical to the success of the implementation efforts: the functionality of a given digital tool itself, pedagogic considerations for that tool, and related classroom-management issues. Chapter 3 goes into considerable detail about the various roles of teachers in classrooms with digital initiatives, but a brief window into expectations around teacher capacity here will help us to understand the embedded assumptions that districts (and vendors) frequently make when envisioning the integration of digital tools.

First, considerable knowledge and skills are required for classroom teachers to understand the functionality of the digital tool itself. This includes managing the enrollment process, logging students in, monitoring use or course completion status, and unlocking content. We saw one teacher in DISD successfully navigate the dual roles of technical assistance support and classroom management by counting aloud in Spanish the number of people logged into a tablet-based program, minimizing the amount of time students spent transitioning from one interface to another.

Second, beyond the functionality of the tool, teachers have to understand how to integrate it instructionally. Some did this quite well. In one DISD classroom, a teacher walked around and monitored students as they worked independently. The teacher stopped to have individual conversations with most students, spending the most time with six students in a semicircle at the front of the room. The lesson incorporated assessment and practice problems, after which students switched to Reasoning Minds City, an online tool for blended learning in math. When students finished their test and a set of practice problems through the online system, the teacher came over to discuss how each student did individually.

In another example, an MPS teacher described how although the credit-recovery course program consisted of self-contained instructional modules, there were times when instructors needed to draw on instructional resources to fill in the gap. For instance, in science classes, the teachers were expected to conduct live labs with students to supplement the online materials. However, the teachers did not have the equipment (Bunsen burners, test tubes, etc.), let alone the staffing, to safely undertake the labs with their students. Thus, their solution or compromise was to have students look up the labs on YouTube and watch them instead.

Lastly, districts and vendors assume a level of teacher capacity for classroom management and student engagement that is specific to the district's digital learning initiatives. In MPS's online credit-recovery classes, many instructors talked about how their primary role shifted from teaching course content to a focus on motivating students to finish courses. They concentrated their efforts on creating systems that enabled them to monitor student activity in the classrooms, to report back to students on their progress, and to generate incentives for students to continue working toward completion of their courses. One teacher accomplished this by making a list of students "in the red" who probably wouldn't be able to finish a course before the end of the semester. At the beginning of the class, the teacher asked if they wanted to work after class, volunteering to be email accessible for questions and to unlock courses until 9:00 p.m. The teacher asked the class, "Who's going to pass a class today?" He checked in with individual students to amp up their engagement and see if they were going to be able to be productive where they were sitting.

Given the broad range of knowledge and skills needed for educators to implement digital tools in the classroom, professional development becomes imperative. However, the support offered by the vendors of digital tools is typically limited to the technical properties of the technology. For example, in one of our study districts, we observed three separate professional development workshops provided by a vendor for classroom teachers. The content of these trainings focused on the mechanics of how the tool worked (e.g., enrolling students, setting up coursework, tracking completion) and, for the teachers more experienced with the tool, how to pull in additional content from outside the platform. It was incumbent on the district to develop customized, more regular trainings for teachers to be offered throughout the school year, including information on district expectations and policies governing implementation and the sharing out best practices across classrooms.

District Organizational Processes

In addition to capacity-related expectations, district beliefs about organizational processes, including decision making, contracting, scaling, communications, and access to data, also shape their implementation of digital learning initiatives. We discuss below some of the critical factors that districts need to address as schools implement online learning programs.

Procurement of Digital Tools

As with the implementation of any major initiative to transform how students learn, school districts need to establish processes that ensure initial buy-in of school-level staff and that support the initiatives' implementation and sustainability. The first among these is the decision-making process about which digital tools to adopt, and for which students and course subjects. Who is invited to participate in these decision-making processes? It matters whether decision making is centralized (i.e., district-level) or decentralized (i.e. school-based), and whether it is top-down (e.g., large-scale software purchase at the district level) or ground-up (e.g., expressed need of classroom teachers and students with input into the digital tools considered). For example, does a digital learning initiative consider and interact directly with a given school's improvement plans, or does a school feel stuck with a cache of devices that the district purchased and expects them to figure out how to use effectively? In DISD, which first started with 1:1 laptops in rolling out its digital learning program, teachers found that the greater storage and technical capacity for running applications on laptops (versus tablets) did not necessarily benefit students, who found it more challenging to stay on task with the expanded options. It was important for teachers to have a feedback loop in the decision-making process about which digital tool the district should go with as it continued to expand the program.

Contracting with Vendors

The contracting process in districts can have an outsized impact on how digital initiatives roll out, given districts' key role in determining the costs and supports that will be in place to support their implementation. In larger districts, purchases of digital software and programs are typically managed by a procurement office in consultation with relevant departments (e.g., Curriculum and Instruction, Technology and Innovation). What types of information do those in charge of the contracting and procurement process gather from across the district to ensure that the resources available for technology integration will be adequate? The extent to which both administrators and classroom teachers have input into the writing of an RFP and the subsequent decision of which vendor or program should be awarded a contract can matter greatly to implementation.

In addition, local educational agencies making technology purchases can use their leverage at the time of contracting and procurement to require vendors to specify how the vendors will work with the district to facilitate the success of their digital learning program. These contract specifications can include:

- Details on the digital tools' scope and capabilities for instruction, and how the vendor will support their performance and management in schools and classrooms
- A commitment to providing equal access and adaptations for all students, including English language learners and students with special educational needs (abilities and disabilities)
- Provision of training and ongoing capacity building to enable school staff to use digital tools equitably and effectively in increasing student achievement
- Stipulations to provide training and support services to aid school-based staff in addressing common technical problems that regularly arise
- An agreement that vendors will share with the school district data that they collect on student use of the education technology and teacher participation in vendor-provided training for the district's own analysis and use in process improvement

Districts would also benefit from networking with other districts using the same digital tools, so that they can share information on vendor contracts and work collectively to increase the benefits realized by schools and their students in the procurement and integration of digital tools.

Scaling Up Digital Learning Initiatives

Some digital initiatives begin with a pilot phase or gradually roll out devices within schools (or across schools or grade levels) in the district to ensure that the tools are serving the teachers and students as intended. How and when districts determine that digital learning efforts are going well and worth expanding is as important as the processes they develop for scaling the program. How is the district engaging stakeholders—school-based staff, teachers, students, parents and any partners in technology integration—in the evaluation process? Have plans been created to gather feedback and insights from users in both successful and lagging sites to inform the nature and pace of the scaling process? For example, in DISD, we found that the same professional development process might be meeting the needs of teachers and staff at one school, while another school lacking support and facilitation for teacher professional development for technology integration might require an alternative approach to ensure that teachers are prepared for an expansion of the digital learning initiative. Because capacities for scaling the implementation of digital tools will often vary across schools, it is critical for district leadership to take the time to collect and understand information on their readiness and the factors that are likely to support or stymie scaling in schools before launching the next phase.

Communication and Evaluation

The communication process around the implementation of digital initiatives is a critical factor influencing the trajectory of technology integration. Districts should explore and activate all avenues of communication (both frequency and nature) between the vendor, district (e.g., contract offices, planners, tech support), school staff (e.g., administrators and classroom teachers), and users (e.g., teachers and students) of digital tools. It also is important to be purposeful about how the goals and expectations for use of digital tools are communicated with parents and caregivers of students served. With many digital tools designed for use both during and outside the school day, family and community members will also often have important roles to play in supporting students' success in learning with them.

Lastly, school districts also need to consider this diversity of stakeholders when they are putting policies into place regarding who has access to information on classroom- and student-level use of digital tools (administrators, teachers, parents, students, etc.) and how these data are used to track, evaluate, and guide student progress. For example, should parents be able to access progress reports through their own log-in credentials, or should they have to depend on accessing this information through teachers and their children? In addition to formative uses of data, what resources are available and processes in place for districts and schools to take a more summative look at the impact of digital tools on student-level outcomes? As we noted above, districts can specify in their contracting processes with vendors requirements that they provide access to data that can be used in independent evaluations, as MPS did with its ed-tech vendors. Districts should also consider whether to allow researchers/evaluators access to student records maintained by the district and to enable the linking of these data to those from the vendors' digital archives. We found over and over in our work with our district partners that in the absence of data from the districts to link to vendor records, looking at the vendor data alone would have told a very different story of how the digital tools were serving the needs of students and the schools in the district than that we see in our collaborative evaluation efforts.

Supporting Liftoff: Ideas for How Districts and States Can Support Successful Rollout of Digital Tools

No two classrooms are alike, and schools often are their own microclimates within a larger school district ecosystem. Therefore, many of the decisions about how to best implement digital tools should be made at, or in concert with, the school and classroom levels. The role of districts and states should primarily be to set up schools and classrooms for success in making these decisions. What can districts do to ensure the conditions for successful rollout, especially in low-resource settings? What parts of existing structures and processes should be kept and aligned to digital learning initiatives, and which should be fundamentally changed to better support their rollout? Our work with multiple districts as they worked through the messiness of implementing digital tools in classrooms suggests four areas districts should consider in supporting liftoff: needs and goals, capacity, organizational processes, and organizational cultures.

Understanding Needs and Goals

A systematic look at the needs and goals of the district should precede the purchase of digital tools. In other words, don't let the tools drive your understanding of your needs. The market offers incredible digital tools with remarkable features, few of which educators in your schools or the students you serve may truly need. Districts should also do a systematic assessment of both the overall goals for stakeholders as well as their specific needs, and this should be done before talking with specific vendors of digital learning products. We found that there often were different perceptions and interpretations across stakeholders of the goals of digital initiatives. For example, both explicit and implicit goals emerged through examination of an online credit-recovery program in Milwaukee. The explicit goal was for students to recover credit and therefore improve their chances of graduating. This goal was written on boards in classrooms, discussed by teachers in interviews, and emphasized in how the program measures success. Learning the content itself was less often mentioned as an explicit goal, yet it emerged that an implicit goal of the online course-taking program was that it provided a safe space for students who otherwise might not be in school at all. This theme came out in interviews and observations, where lab instructors were managing the intersection of their classroom with the complicated lives of the students with whom they worked. One teacher said that if there is a kid making progress, she does not harass that student: "This lab becomes a place for EBD (emotional and behavioral disorder) students to decompress for a period so they are better able to deal with their other classes." The instructor was fine with this situation as long as she wasn't going to be held accountable by district administration to have students finish courses. Differences in perspectives are expected and normal, but they also should be accounted for when planning and evaluating the effectiveness of digital learning initiatives, as they factor into how stakeholders buy into and support the initiatives.

While there are a number of tools and strategies for doing needs assessments, ideally, any assessment of goals and needs should purposefully engage the voices of end users, particularly students and their teachers. Youth and educators offer nuanced perspectives on the conditions for implementation, as well as a window into what their own motivation might be in using digital tools. Similarly, districts should find ways to systematically collect ongoing feedback from end users, especially in the first stages of implementation. For example, we partnered with one of our study districts to do a daylong summer workshop with teachers who were experienced users of a particular digital tool. The objectives of the session were to: (1) review and co-interpret findings from our research on the tool, and (2) identify high-leverage practices in the implementation of the tool in their classrooms. Practices identified as most important included those related to how to systematically track progress in ways that were meaningful to the student, how to manage the presence of cell phones in the classrooms, and creative ways to recognize and motivate students as they hit milestones in the coursework.

Understanding Organizational and Individual Capacity

Digital tools are not rolled out in a vacuum. They come into already existing situations that can either facilitate integration or create barriers. Similar to mapping needs and goals, districts should map the current capacities and assets of organizations (the district, schools, vendors, community-based partners) and individuals (school-level administrators, classroom teachers, support staff, students, and families) involved in implementation. The organizational capacity of the district, schools, and even community partners involved in student learning (e.g., community library, afterschool programs) is critical to maximizing their potential to support student learning both during and outside the school day. Educators and administrators looking to implement digital learning initiatives should systematically map available facilities (e.g., computer labs), internet connectivity, and available hardware (e.g., computers, projectors). Once digital learning is launched, they also need tools and strategies to monitor their implementation. For example, in collaboration with both of our district partners, we created a Classroom Walk-Through Instrument (see appendix B) to aid district staff in collecting descriptive data on digital instructional tool use in schools and classrooms, to develop school-level profiles on their implementation, and to assess how existing practices align with the goals of the initiatives. Districts should also consider the capacity of the digital tools themselves, such as: Do certain tools work only with certain populations or with certain pedagogic approaches? As districts map and plan for funding streams for both short- and long-term technology integration efforts, they should also factor in the importance of resources for ongoing monitoring and evaluation that can help them get on the best path to realizing the promise of their digital learning programs.

Understanding Organizational Processes

In addition to understanding needs, goals, and capacities, districts also need to have a clear sense of the processes in place that impact the implementation of digital tools. As organizations, districts rely heavily on entrenched processes to communicate and evaluate the work done in schools. Before launching digital learning efforts, and recognizing that inclusive decision making is likely to be key to buy-in for diverse stakeholders, districts should first consider whether their existing processes are structured to support their success. For example, are they top-down or democratic? Who drives the decisions, and how decentralized is governance? Second, what are the informal and formal avenues for communication between the district and end-users? Is it ad hoc and as needed, or systematic and designed to uncover issues below the surface? Third, given that most districts contract for the digital learning tools used in their classrooms, the entire contracting process (from the RFP to getting the final vendor report) should be designed to minimize complexity and opacity and should build in opportunities for review of outcomes to ensure that the goals of the digital learning initiatives are being achieved. In their book *Equal Scrutiny*, Patricia Burch and Annalee Good also recommend making explicit in the contracts what (or who) drives assessment and access to data and how districts and their vendors will ensure that commercial or political interests don't trump the best interests of the students they serve.[6]

Understanding Organizational Cultures

Even with well-trained staff and seamless communication protocols in place, digital learning initiatives still can fail to launch when a supportive organizational culture is lacking. For example, given the often turbulent nature of low-resource districts (e.g., high turnover, politicized policy climate, recurring budget cuts), what is the current tolerance for change? What is the role of youth and family voice in the organizational culture? Is there a culture of technology integration in the district office—that is, is technology an assumed part of how the district office itself works? How do the district and schools interact with their partners in evaluation and research? More generally, what processes do districts have in place for managing and maintaining productive relationships between all partners and stakeholders engaged in implementing, scaling, and evaluating digital learning programs?

This chapter has focused on policies, conditions, and assumptions at state and district levels that most influence the implementation and effectiveness of digital learning initiatives. Chapter 3 goes into greater detail in describing the instructional setting for digital tools at the classroom level, including the role of teachers in implementation, the nature of teacher-student relationships in digital learning, and particular considerations for classrooms in low-resource settings that are striving to better serve historically marginalized students.

3

Unlocking Successful Technology Integration in the Classroom

To understand the promise and challenges of digital learning, we must dig deep into the experiences of teachers and students in the classroom. Indeed, one of the most consistent findings in the research on school effectiveness is the vital role of teachers in improving student learning, and this includes technology-enhanced instruction. At the same time, the introduction of digital learning opportunities alters the integral role of the instructor, and often where instruction takes place. This, in turn, generates new demands on instructor capacities—what they need to know and are expected to do in the classroom. Instructors' capacity to enact and optimize digital tools is critical in shaping how and to what the extent digital learning will transform the classroom teaching and learning experience.

To be effective, technology integration in the classroom should not be a solitary journey for teachers, but rather a collaborative endeavor that draws on the support of district- and school-level administrators, fellow teachers, and the teacher's students and their families. Supports for building instructor capacity to effectively use digital tools should—*at a minimum*—include technology training and ongoing access to professional development, hands-on practice calibrated to each teachers' skills and instructional context, and opportunities for collaboration with other instructors.[1] The realities of digital learning in the school and classroom often differ drastically, however, from the test case imagined and sold by technology program developers. Technology developers rarely encounter firsthand the resource inadequacies that public schools regularly reckon with; the time and scheduling constraints that limit development of the breadth and depth of technical skill and pedagogical knowledge required; challenges with student engagement in the classroom; or competing instructional demands. For example, in one observation, students were asked complete an assignment using Kindles. The instructor was the only person there to sort through technical glitches, and the classroom was so chaotic that he was constantly turning around to deal with another problem. The operability of the devices wasn't in question as much as logging into the software. One student didn't have a Kindle the entire time and was left to sit by himself. This extreme example of how resource constraints can limit technology use as well as instructional time and student learning shows explicitly that while digital tools can enhance instructional activities, they can also detract from the learning environment if teachers are not sufficiently supported in their use.

This chapter focuses our investigation of digital instruction on the classroom level. We aim to extend typical discussions of instructor capacity needs, professional development design, and tech support delivery to an examination of the unique challenges and opportunities of digital learning in low-resource contexts with historically marginalized student populations. Our findings and the examples that follow will illuminate the experiences of teachers and students in two large, urban school districts in high-poverty settings.

The Role of the Teacher in Digital Learning-Based Instructional Models

Both technology vendors and district administrators consistently point to the critical role of instructor capacity—knowledge, skills, and attitudes—

in enacting and realizing the potential of digital learning tools in public elementary and secondary schools. Although students often are envisioned as "co-creators" of their learning experiences and as actively choosing *how* they learn and progress through digital content, it also is clear that instructors are expected to strongly support students in tailoring learning to their particular strengths and needs and ensuring that they master the content at appropriate levels or standards.[2] Yet, teachers' varying capacities for technology integration can limit this potential and students' subsequent access to quality educational opportunities. Below, we briefly describe the diversity of digital learning–based instructional models and teacher roles within our sample before discussing the challenges of building and allocating instructor capacity in low-resource schools.

Shifting Instructional Models and Teacher Roles

Technology integration takes various forms based on the nature, capacities, educational context, and intended uses of digital tools. Students' use of stand-alone online course software, for example, fundamentally shifts the role of the teacher away from content development and delivery. While not as dramatic, other uses of instructional technology such as personalized learning may also shift the primary instructional and administrative functions a teacher performs. For instance, we observed that internet-enabled tablets allowed teachers to redirect time from one-size-fits-all, whole-classroom instruction to differentiating and facilitating student learning in small groups, as in the following elementary classroom instructional session:

> The classroom was laid out in four clustered stations of desks, of which two were in constant, rotating use. Another u-shaped cluster around the teacher's desk provided a station for small-group instruction. Students worked diligently on their assignment individually and in small groups. Students were teaching each other after having worked with the instructor. The movement of students between stations was crisp and without delay. When students completed their rotations, they were assessed on a problem set. They worked on this quietly and individually, while the instructor rotated around the room to gauge progress and set up the laptop to project answers to the questions.

Technology integration requires teachers in settings such as the one described above to develop not only the technical expertise to manage device usage in their classrooms, but also the skills to promote and support new student-centered learning strategies. Professional development aimed at only the added technical demands on students and teachers will fail to adequately prepare technology enactors to realize the full benefits of its use.

Across the range of digital learning programs, we identified persistent challenges to cultivating the strong instructional background and supports needed for many of the most effective uses of instructional technology. Although we relatively infrequently observed truly blended instruction—that is, teachers and students working together to choose instruction and implement learning strategies using face-to-face *and* technology-based models—research indicates that students achieve at higher levels when technology is delivered in blended learning environments.[3] In addition to innovative curriculum structures and instructional models, truly transformative digital learning models engage students through adapting to individual student contexts, needs, and abilities *in ways that would not be possible without technology*. The most effective use of digital learning often requires more and different, not less, investment from teachers. Accordingly, to pave the way for greater success in technology integration, it is essential to consider and plan for how expectations of teachers' roles and responsibilities will change when introducing technology into the classroom.

The broad spectrum of instructor roles in enacting digital learning— from a minimal role focused on classroom supervision and device management to more innovative and highly involved instructional roles—is influenced by a range of factors across diverse settings. In fact, even when observing the same digital learning tool for the same intended population of users in the same school, we sometimes saw very different instructor approaches to guiding digital learning. The following are some of the most common instructor roles we observed in our study schools:

- Completing *administrative responsibilities* to enroll or assist students in initiating and progressing through instruction by manag-

ing the program interface (e.g., troubleshooting log-in problems, facilitating assessment capabilities of the tool)
- Providing *technical support* in the instructional environment
- *Monitoring and redirecting student behavior* to keep technology users on task
- *Supporting student engagement in learning* (e.g., motivating, building relationships, counseling)
- Utilizing software to *monitor or assess student progression and knowledge*
- Proving *instructional support*, including direct and blended instruction, content assistance, and differentiated instruction

Figure 3.1 groups these roles into categories and identifies the frequency with which we observed them across the digital learning programs in our study. In enacting online course-taking, which is frequently used by high school students in Milwaukee Public Schools (MPS) for credit recovery, we saw instructors primarily attending to administrative responsibilities; relatively few interacted with the online learning tool in ways that supported content learning. Most teachers defined their role as motivating students to progress through the instructional interface in their online courses, addressing technical issues, and carrying out administrative responsibilities such as entering student permissions to retake a quiz in the system. Less often, teachers provided instructional support to individual students who asked for help on the content of the course itself.

The following vignette illustrates a frequently observed role of instructors in a high school online credit-recovery classroom:

> The teacher was checking in/greeting the students, answering phones/doors, making sure students were working in the online instructional program instead of checking on cell phones. The teacher stopped by a couple of times to check the progress of one of the students. When the student got up to ask the teacher to review the quiz, the teacher told him to go back and review. The student came back to the computer, looked at the notes again, toggled between problems, fiddled with his paper. He stayed on the same problem for five minutes, possibly waiting for the teacher to check it again. The teacher came over and asked him if he

Figure 3.1

Instructor roles performed by program

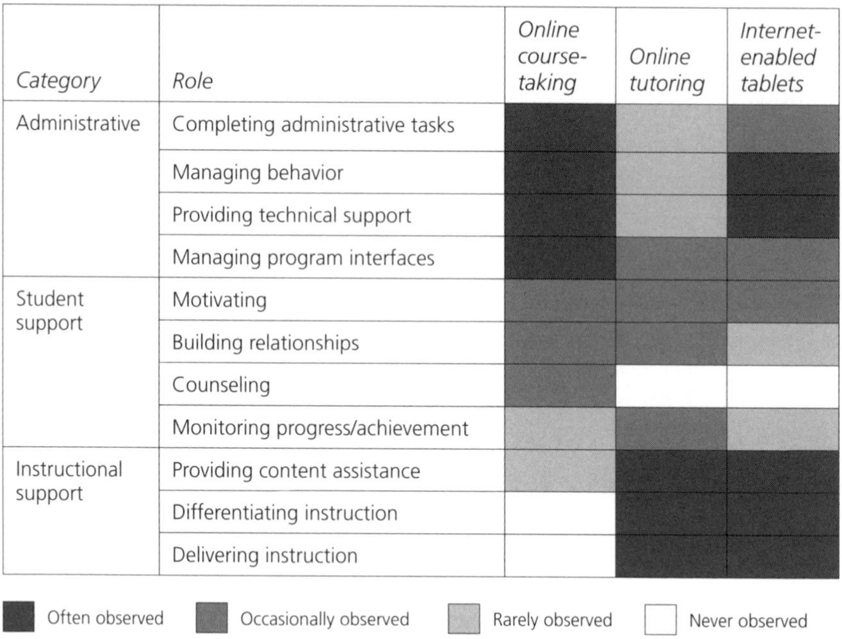

Category	Role	Online course-taking	Online tutoring	Internet-enabled tablets
Administrative	Completing administrative tasks	Often	Rarely	Often
	Managing behavior	Often	Rarely	Often
	Providing technical support	Often	Rarely	Often
	Managing program interfaces	Often	Often	Often
Student support	Motivating	Occasionally	Often	Often
	Building relationships	Occasionally	Often	Rarely
	Counseling	Occasionally	Never	Never
	Monitoring progress/achievement	Rarely	Occasionally	Often
Instructional support	Providing content assistance	Rarely	Often	Often
	Differentiating instruction	Never	Often	Often
	Delivering instruction	Never	Often	Often

■ Often observed ■ Occasionally observed ■ Rarely observed □ Never observed

needed a check, which the student said he did. Then the teacher came over and told the student which problems to fix. He then submitted the quiz and went onto the next part of the course.

The example above is representative of how we saw teachers interacting with this particular online learning tool—not in ways that supported content learning, but rather reviewing students' work for accuracy and guiding students toward passing assessments. Alternatively, in some contexts, teachers took advantage of this type of asynchronous, technology-driven instruction in online course-taking: as the tool reduced their traditional teaching responsibilities, they used the extra time to perform roles such as motivating and counseling students and encouraging their engagement in the learning process.

In contrast, the online tutoring program for elementary students in Milwaukee, which delivered instruction entirely through an online platform outside the regular school day, minimized administrative tasks and was intended to facilitate a one-to-one or two-to-one student-to-teacher ratio (see again figure 3.1). The structure of the tutoring sessions encouraged a focus on content and enabled opportunities for individualized instruction and somewhat targeted interventions, with occasional time for student support such as building rapport and student confidence. Due to the relatively small number of students for whom a given instructor was responsible, instructors also spent less time devoted to administrative roles, technical support, and behavior management.

Falling somewhere between these two paradigms, teacher roles in the integration of internet-enabled tablets in elementary classrooms in the Dallas Independent School District were more varied and demanding, with teachers expected to perform both administrative and instructional roles, often at the same time (the final column of figure 3.1). In addition to integrating digital learning programs that provided differentiated lessons and practice, teachers also used technology-driven instruction to reallocate their time from direct instruction to differentiating or personalizing educational experiences for students. The tablets provided an advantage in offering a menu of educational software options that could be incorporated into lessons. However, the diversity of choices, as well as the opportunity to decide how and how often to use them, made teacher knowledge and skills both more critical and challenging (compared with contexts where instructors had to become adept at supporting only a single program). How teachers enacted these roles in practice—for example, the extent to which they differentiated instruction or employed blended learning strategies—depended heavily on the platform itself and individual instructor capacity (typically gained through experience or prior professional development), but also on student, classroom, and environmental factors. The following vignette shows how one instructor turned a challenging classroom circumstance—an unexpected near-doubling of his class size because of another teacher's absence—into a successful learning experience through blended instruction and varied use of tablets:

> Students were entering the room and picking up tablets. Students were coming in from another classroom, too, so the physical environment was especially crowded. The teacher effectively worked through this

limitation, using pairing and small groups to facilitate learning. He gave the students five minutes to practice their vocabulary and told students to quiz each other, which they did; he had a five-minute timer projected on the screen. The instructor moved around the room, checking on students and encouraging them. The students were quizzing each other on the meaning/translation of vocabulary words (Spanish to English and vice versa). The students logged into Quizlet Live, and the instructor logged in at the front of the room (on the screen). The students were placed into groups and worked together to answer the questions projected on the screen (they needed to match words and definitions, putting their tablets together). In the whole-group instruction that followed, they examined character interactions in the literature. They continued pair-sharing times, where the instructor would pose questions to students and ask them to discuss them with a partner.

In this exceptional example of blended learning, the students were offered variety and the opportunity to interact, collaborate, and co-create their learning experiences, while the instructor simultaneously interacted with them in content learning and encouraged and supported their engagement with the lesson and each other.

Redefining the Student-Teacher Relationship

With digital learning often reducing student-teacher interactions devoted to direct instruction, teacher discretion, classroom environment, and student needs predictably dictate how that time is used and whether teachers maintain similar levels of interactions with students, even as the content of those interactions may change. Below, we highlight evidence indicating the importance of student-teacher relationship development for effective technology integration, particularly in classroom environments where interactions around course content are otherwise limited.

Developing a Sense of Belonging

Teachers play a key role in developing a supportive learning environment regardless of the level of digital learning occurring. However, the classroom environment can play an even larger role in student progress when instruction relies on student-directed learning and for students who may have struggled to stay on track in school in the past.[4] We observed that some teachers create a supportive classroom environment by engaging in relationship-building interactions with students and offering encouragement and counseling, as well as volunteering time outside of the school day to assist students in completing course content. In interviews, teachers discussed the importance of providing students with non-academic, as well as academic, support. One instructor explained, "I'm their administrator, counselor, and teacher." As a teacher supporting students enrolled in online credit-recovery courses, this teacher found himself counseling the students least engaged in learning, which stemmed from a host of reasons. He recounted one example of a student who came into class crying because her grandmother had been shot over the weekend. The student needed to talk about the experience before being ready to engage in instruction. We observed and heard numerous other instances where students discussed life stressors with teachers.

Although at first glance, it might be a concern that personal versus academically focused conversations will detract from instructional time, research indicates that demonstrating an interest in students' lives is an essential first step toward earning their trust.[5] And developing that trust is critical to students feeling a part of and committed to learning in a classroom. Further, providing a supportive, caring learning environment encourages both help-seeking and engagement, two critical components of success in digital learning.[6] In a traditional, face-to-face classroom setting, teachers often have to choose between addressing concerns such as the one above and delivering whole-group instruction, while technology-driven instruction in some classroom environments and configurations afforded instructors the time to attend to students more holistically. This shift may be particularly important for students who may be alienated by or otherwise disengaged from school.

Unfortunately, despite the need for holistic supports among many students in our study districts, we observed relatively few instructors integrating relationship-building and other nonacademic supports with technology-driven instruction. These practices can be encouraged by providing teachers with resources and guidance in generating strategies for developing supportive student-teacher relationships, ideally as part of a comprehensive professional development and support program. At the same time, not all teachers will be well suited to or see it as their responsibility to take on additional roles of counselor or confidant in the classroom, so school-based supports for serving these student needs will inevitably be critical as well.

Using Data to Personalize Assistance to Students

Education technology vendors tout the advantages that digital tools offer teachers in accessing real-time data on how students are using the tool, tailoring instructional programming, and targeting assistance to students not making adequate progress in their courses or other learning.[7] This likewise requires the development of new capacities for data management and analysis by instructors, as well as time during classroom periods to monitor and engage with students about what the data indicate about their educational progress and needs. Sometimes, although not always, we observed how formative assessments and other program analytics helped to facilitate student engagement or provide information to teachers for individualizing instruction. One example of this was the use of ALL In Learning clickers to quickly measure student understanding. When using these clickers or similar tools, students could record their answers to questions posed to the class. The teacher saw students' answers and how long it took them to respond. Importantly, when students did not demonstrate mastery, the teacher used information from the quiz as an opportunity to provide peer assistance and re-teaching. In another classroom observation, an instructor used the Kahoot! app to administer a teacher-generated quiz. Afterward, the teacher led a quick discussion that responded to the cumulative class results before he pulled three students requiring additional assistance out from digital instruction, while the rest of the students progressed at their own pace through teacher-generated online games and quizzes using the Kahoot! platform.

In addition to in-person interventions, the teacher that deployed the Kahoot! app also made modifications to how students interacted with the digital program. In contrast, when teachers didn't leverage available information on progress from student use of digital tools, they were less likely to re-teach material or give students more opportunities to practice underlying skills. Furthermore, we have found that when teachers don't have access to (or don't use) the information on student progress provided by digital programs, they are instead more likely to rely on student signals and requests for help, which can exacerbate existing patterns of inequality, as students with more positive learner identities and with more comfort in dominant cultural settings are more likely to demand or even monopolize teacher attention.[8]

Using Data to Personalize Students' Goal-Setting

In some high school classrooms, we observed teachers meeting individually with students to set and discuss their progress towards goals within the online program, drawing on progress monitoring reports provided through the online course system. Through setting goals in conjunction with weekly one-on-one student-teacher check-ins, teachers provided students with regular feedback aimed at creating manageable goals and helping students develop self-regulation strategies needed to succeed in a technology-driven instructional environment. Some teachers supplemented online feedback by tracking and encouraging student progress toward goals using paper charts and incentives like certificates or rewards; in fact, some of these strategies were fairly creative. For example, one teacher described how he tapped student interest in college basketball's "March Madness" to create teams and brackets where students competed to achieve the highest average team progress toward completing their online courses. Regular check-ins also facilitated more consistent communication about expectations for student educational progress and allowed teachers to identify when students required more in-person and one-on-one assistance.

Equity Implications of Time Reallocation

While enabling teachers to reallocate time from direct instruction toward more targeted, individualized, or small-group assistance is often promoted as a strength of digital learning, teachers' choices of how this time is allocated can have profound implications for the quality of students' educational experiences. For example, in a Dallas elementary classroom using internet-enabled tablets, we saw the potential for inequitable distribution of instructor time to exacerbate opportunity gaps when the instructor worked with a small group on math activities but left the majority of the students to complete worksheets on their own. Six students received personalized teacher attention, while the majority lost interest in the worksheet-like digital instruction and turned to distracting and bothering each other, squandering considerable classroom learning time. In contrast, the teacher in the following example made an effort to speak to each student individually, instead of only responding to those students who requested assistance or those assigned to small-group instruction:

> The teacher walks around and monitors as students work independently. She has individual conversations with most students. The teacher spends more time with the six students in a semicircle at the front of the room but monitors the others . . . When students finish their test and a set of practice problems, the teacher comes by and discusses how they did.

As discussed above, technology use in the classroom frequently reduces the extent to which a teacher is responsible for direct instruction, but more often than not, teachers appeared to be unaware of the equity implications of the choices they were making in allocating their time in the classroom. It is also possible that in some cases, teachers were indifferent to concerns about differential student access to quality educational opportunities. For example, this teacher in a high school online learning lab in MPS appeared apathetic toward students, even when they called out for assistance:

> For about the first ten minutes of the period, the instructor worked to get students logged into their Chromebooks and working. The noise at the back of the room where the students were just talking and goofing around was growing. About half of the class was very disruptive. One student called out to the teacher and said, "I don't know how to use this." The teacher did not respond. She sat at the front of the room and

didn't make an effort to engage the students who weren't doing anything. A half-hour into the period, only two students were still working.

Clear expectations regarding an instructor's role and responsibilities in integrating technology *for all students* is an essential first step toward realizing an equitable distribution of the benefits of technology integration for student learning. Yet in situations or classroom environments, such as the one described above, it is apparent teachers need specific and sustained training that goes beyond just technology integration to also address equity and inclusion issues.

Factors Influencing Teacher Roles and Practices in Technology Integration

Our research explored how teacher capacity interacted with other, related factors—such as the reliability of technology, student characteristics, the classroom environment, and teacher beliefs regarding the efficacy of the technology—to influence the intensity with which teachers used technology, how they enacted digital learning in the classroom, and student outcomes. We drew on the full range of data collected in our study in exploring connections between instructional practices and structural factors. Our analyses of classroom observation and teacher interview and survey data identified the following key factors for effectively leveraging technology to promote classroom learning:

- *Technology functioning and teacher technical knowledge for supporting digital tool use* are critical for avoiding glitches and lags that reduce instructional time and constrain more innovative teaching practices.
- Teachers' *baseline technology expertise and subsequent growth in their expertise* from the beginning to the end of the school year are positively associated with student engagement and achievement gains through technology use.
- Particularly in technology-directed environments, *program features* play a substantial role in shaping student experiences. Teachers in the most successful classrooms understand how to best leverage the strengths and supplement the limitations of these features.

- In teacher-directed environments, *teacher beliefs* in the efficacy of technology for student learning increase their use of blended instruction and the overall intensity of technology use in the classroom.
- Third-party digital learning–based tools and programs often require *intensive accommodations and supplements* predicated on blended instructional techniques to meet the instructional needs and educational realities of students attending low-resource schools.

These findings suggest that in planning and implementing technology initiatives, schools need to consider the interrelatedness of educational context and teacher capacity and the ongoing feedback loop between the implementation process, teacher beliefs and experience, and their technology integration practices in the classroom. Each component and relevant policy implications are discussed in greater detail below.

Cultivate Sufficient Technology Infrastructure

As discussed in chapter 2, access to functional technology is key to maximizing teacher time and capacity for enacting more innovative instructional practices (e.g., blended instruction) in the classroom, as well as for increasing the level of student support they can provide when implementing digital learning.[9] Prior research suggests that in the face of inadequate and underfunded technology infrastructure and supports, technology use is more likely to involve lower-order, "drill and practice" activities rather than higher-order, skills-building classroom work.[10] But even well-planned, blended lessons can be disrupted by technical glitches, as in this extended illustration of a DISD elementary classroom:

> Students opened Brain Pop Junior, and the teacher instructed them to go to "Movie of the Week." The teacher began leading the students in group instruction, but then she realized that the tablets were not opening for most students (only six students initially got on and could go to the writing skills area as instructed; the messages they were getting were "The movie did not load" or "Unable to load; please check your network connection"). Ten minutes later, most students were now on a

device or sharing a device, and the teacher told them to watch a movie about nouns, although she was still troubleshooting devices. Some students watched the movie without headphones because they were sharing devices. The teacher then asked the students to turn to the writing component. The students were supposed to use QR codes to get a "personal narrative rubric" and to write a composition. They rolled a die to select a QR code from the six options, and then scanned that code to get the writing prompt. Most students only had about five minutes for writing; the technology problems appeared to have cost them about ten minutes of writing time.

In other observations, teachers requested the assistance of technical support personnel to troubleshoot challenges, and we also observed students assisting fellow classmates. With greater technical capacity required with increased access to a wider array of tools, programs, and resources, teachers sometimes experienced technical issues that they were unable to resolve on their own. Although in DISD, the Jiv Daya Foundation provided technical support for tablet integration via phone, the resolution of more challenging technical issues required placing a request with the central district technical support team. Even an emergency request for assistance involved waiting for technology support personnel to drive to the school; thus there was often disparate access to quality educational experiences for students based on the technical expertise of their teacher. Furthermore, reliance on teachers to solve technical issues as they emerged also limited the teachers' ability to provide face-to-face instruction in the classroom.

At the same time, we also observed a number of strategies our partnering schools developed and employed over time to minimize the impact of technology issues. For instance, the Jiv Daya Foundation found that providing additional tablets to DISD classrooms (above the expected class sizes) in anticipation of charging issues or device failure reduced lost instructional time. At other times, teachers in Dallas replaced inoperable devices with tablets borrowed from other classrooms, while students in both Dallas and Milwaukee often transitioned to other technology in the classroom, such as additional desktop computers or Chromebooks, instead of waiting for assistance to resolve technical issues. Clearly, planning and budgeting for technical problems and device failure can aid in ensuring access to alternative devices and minimizing losses in access to instructional content. In addition, the use of primarily wired, desktop computers for online course-taking in MPS seemed to limit technical difficulties related to wireless connectivity and charging that were experienced in other settings when using tablets and laptops.

Furthermore, when device sharing between students is unavoidable, it does not inevitably result in a diluted instructional experience, but rather can turn out positively, as in the exemplar of blending learning described earlier in this chapter (the teacher whose class size doubled unexpectedly). In fact, we observed that device sharing could sometimes facilitate peer-to-peer learning and collaboration, indicating that a 1:1 student-to-device ratio was not a necessary condition for digital learning. Haßler, Major, and Hennessy suggest that with the relative advantage tablets provide in many low-resource settings, targeting a 1:1 ratio may not be the best use of limited resources.[11] Instead, the same funds might be better used to enhance professional development for teachers on device use and integration. And to more effectively plan for and adapt to circumstances where 1:1 ratios are not possible, it would be advantageous to offer more professional training to teachers on how to leverage tablets for multiple learners working on a single device.

Prioritize the Development of Basic Technology Expertise Among Teachers and Students

With district finances constraining the allocation of funds for technology specialists and supports on campuses, the in-classroom expertise provided by teachers who are proficient technology users can be critical to sustaining and increasing the effectiveness of technology integration. Beyond traditional professional development strategies, which are often costly and have limited success rates, research shows that peer learning and collaboration have the added benefit of transmitting content-specific integration strategies and explicitly linking device use to instructional strategies.[12] After an initial, less successful attempt to implement tablets into pilot schools, the Jiv Daya Foundation in Dallas actively cultivated peer assistance, mentoring, and learning by grouping the rollout of digital learning in clusters of nearby elementary schools ("feeder pattern" schools) in combination with joint and ongoing professional development and a technical support plan. Compared with previous pilot iterations where teachers irregularly integrated digital learning into instruction, we observed higher rates of consistent take-up and device use in the two years following this programmatic shift.

Teacher beliefs and instructional philosophies have been identified as "gatekeepers" to successful technology integration.[13] Yet research also suggests that professional development and classroom experiences are instrumental in influencing beliefs and, in turn, practice.[14] In DISD, data on teacher beliefs regarding whether technology supported student learning in their classrooms showed that teachers with more highly rated classroom environments were more likely to respond favorably about technology use, reiterating the importance of investing in sufficient technology infrastructure, support, *and* professional development. However, an examination of teacher beliefs over multiple years also found that beliefs were malleable, likely influenced by access to surrounding conditions, levels of training and classroom experiences with technology as described above.[15]

Another cost-efficient, timely, and potentially scalable solution for facilitating greater access to educational technology for student learning is providing increased support for peer-to-peer learning and exchange (both among teachers and students). In some schools, teachers worked together to solve technical challenges and relied on tech-savvy teachers in their building for support, a model for collaboration that is supported by research conducted in Danish schools.[16] In other classrooms, teachers cultivated student "technology leaders" who would assist other students, lead explanations of tips and skills, or model something on a device.

Relying on students to assist peers with using technology need not detract from the educational experience of either student mentors or the peers they assist. Rather, recognizing and drawing on students' technical skills can have the added benefit of encouraging teamwork and student enthusiasm for technology use. Further, fostering these types of shared capacities in teachers and students often increases the timeliness of support for technology integration, which is critical to ensuring both quantity and quality of instructional time, with implications, in turn, for classroom management, student engagement, and teacher availability to support learning.

Leverage Program Strengths and Supplement Limitations

Across digital learning programs and contexts, we found that students benefit when teachers have access to program resources that facilitate appropriate modifications of the technology, and both the teacher and student have the capacity to make use of them. For instance, we observed students receiving individualized instruction facilitated by some digital programs. This individualization took several forms not normally available in a traditional classroom setting, including computer-adapted learning, individually targeted pre-testing, and choices regarding what content or skills a student would like to practice. Providing teachers with information on these individualizing features and sufficient time to feel comfortable implementing them can improve differentiation in the classroom without compromising on quality.

However, meeting students' learning needs may be a particular challenge in schools with competing financial demands and persistent resource constraints. Particularly in these contexts, adapting digital tools to meet the needs of individual learners requires educators to take an active role in selecting, configuring, and adapting programs developed by external vendors. One of the most common challenges educators in our study encountered was the presumed level of self-regulation in students. This expectation was particularly apparent in technology-based digital learning tools that allowed students to work at their own pace with minimal teacher supervision. If scaffolded appropriately, the use of these programs in moderation can assist students in developing self-regulation and other related important life skills. Depending on the context, appropriate scaffolding may include evaluating each students' current level of self-regulation, explicitly teaching self-regulation strategies, setting individualized goals, and providing support, incentives, and recognition for meeting those goals. The instructor in one MPS classroom explained that in each class, when students logged in, they could see their progress; she [the instructor] had a different screen to monitor where they were. Kids checked in with her and set a goal for where they wanted to be. She set a target for them to make 6 percent progress per week and then showed students the resources they had to track their progress. This was the general pattern of goal setting and progress monitoring that we observed in classrooms across the district and highlights how teacher-facilitated and supported use of program features helped students track and receive implicit recognition for course progress.

By establishing measurable, weekly guidelines for student progress such as the 6 percent progress per week measure, educators made expectations for progress more explicit. Students were also more likely to be motivated to achieve these goals when their instructors recognized progress publicly, either through one-on-one meetings, posting completion certificates on whiteboards, or providing small rewards such as food. Other instructors encouraged reengagement and completion by organizing inter- and intra-classroom competitions, such as the college basketball bracket competition described above where students received credit for group completion rates. In addition to motivating students individually, this encouraged group assistance, collaboration, and positive peer engagement.

Prepare Teachers to Provide Intensive Support and Accommodations

In attending to concerns about equity in technology integration, we cannot emphasize enough that most technology vendors design educational applications for use by self-regulated learners performing at grade level.[17] This narrow conception of student users on the part of technology developers presents a host of challenges for teachers of students who do not fit this model. For instance, our analysis and related research shows that student course failures are the single most important factor driving student online course-taking in high school, yet students struggling in the first years of high school and not meeting minimum grade-level guidelines are often set back academically when assigned to online course-taking.[18] Other student populations who may not yet be reading at grade level in the language used by the online program (such as emerging bilingual students or those requiring special education services) need additional, targeted accommodations and modifications from digital learning programs to achieve their full potential. However, these types of purposeful accommodations and modifications were infrequently observed in practice. This MPS teacher represented the views of other instructors when she described how she felt incapable of providing supports that she recognized were needed:

> For some students, the language accommodations in [the online instructional program] are not adequate. Traditional language translations like Italian, German, French, etc., are available in the system, but other languages they need are not: Thai, Burmese, Somali, Arabic, Hindi.

She said some students would work better with the lesson on paper, but she is no longer able to print pages from the online program to give to students. She went to a student's laptop to demonstrate a challenge with the translation function:

> The translation occurs in text [not voice] format, so students have to be able to read the text while the instructor is talking in English. For many students, they understand the spoken language, but they do not know or learn the written language.

Below we further highlight the types of teacher capacity and resources required to integrate and supplement digital learning for three distinct student populations disproportionately present in low-resource school settings: emerging bilingual students, students identified for special education services, and students at risk of not graduating.

Support for Emerging Bilingual Students

The adaptability facilitated by some types of educational technology can be particularly helpful in classrooms where students are learning to communicate in more than one language.[19] For students learning in multiple languages, something as simple as providing access to a set of definitions or personalized reading prompts can expand student access to quality learning experiences. In DISD, where approximately half of all students in pilot schools were learning in bilingual classrooms, we found larger positive effects of tablet use on reading achievement for students in bilingual classrooms; in fact, in classrooms with a higher percentage of emergent bilingual students, we observed increasingly larger effects on student achievement.

Although helpful for all students, research suggests that particularly for emergent bilingual students, teachers—and the professional development made available to them—should emphasize the importance of interactivity and group work within a culturally responsive framework.[20] In the following observations of official bilingual classrooms, teachers combined technology-facilitated instruction with more traditional, interactive teaching strategies to deliver relevant, engaging, discussion-based lessons on science-related topics.

> The instructor relied on the technology to ask students questions, but he drove the content and skill focus with his own implementation of a take on the Socratic method, asking students to explain their answers and understanding of the material (such as asking them to explain why a rock cannot transition to a gaseous state of matter). Each activity sequence was structured, even despite technology obstacles.

> The teacher reads a question in Spanish to students, who must submit their individual answers via e-readers to Kahoot!. A female student discusses how she answered her question, "How does water get into the plant?" She explains in Spanish that the water came from the roots in the ground. The teacher responds with another question (in Spanish) for the students, "How would the chemicals affect the ground and water since chemicals get into the dirt? Do the chemicals affect the plant?" The teacher asks the students to explain their answer in Spanish or English . . .

As these examples show, blended learning can be particularly effective in creating quality learning opportunities for emergent bilingual students. This in-person teacher support contrasts with the limitations of the translation function in the online instructional program described above. The lack of access to consistent instructional supports for ELLs in the lab-style, online learning classrooms in Milwaukee also seriously limited equitable access for all students. Access to a teacher certified to provide ESL instruction and with experience teaching in a bilingual classroom was critical in Dallas to ensuring that digital devices and programs targeted students at appropriate reading and English language proficiency levels.

Support for Students with Special Education Needs

Most digital learning programs provide at least basic accommodations that can assist students with certain types of learning disabilities. Across the settings we observed, technology-based lessons often included audio, which allowed students with certain disabilities, such as dyslexia, to access learning material. Beyond audio, it is easier to enlarge content electronically than when in physical form. In an interview, a teacher described options available in some digital learning–based programs to lower the reading level, which can provide scaffolding for students with certain learning disabilities:

> Students with disabilities utilize the text-to-speech feature within the online instructional program to have passages read to them. I have a few students with disabilities that also utilize a special monitor that enlarges the text and images. Additional resources that I have provided offline for students with disabilities include reducing the number of choices on multiple-choice assessments, passages at lower reading levels, and step-by-step solution guides for the Algebra 1 and Geometry courses.

Highlighting these features and making sure teachers have the skills to implement them can improve student access to educational content. Alternatively, another teacher describing options for accommodating a special education student reading at grade level 2.4 in the same online instructional program explained that the program "cannot accommodate her needs." For other students reading below grade level, she had determined that it was better to have the program settings on "automatic progression," which allowed students to move onto the next lesson even if they failed the prior lesson quiz; otherwise, students would get stuck or wouldn't want to let the teacher know that they had failed a quiz (and needed it to be reset to take it again).

More generally, we observed limited options for more intensive accommodations. In most instances, the differentiation required for students with special needs is left to in-person teachers to facilitate, but instructors supervising labs devoted to online course-taking reported that they rarely had access to information on student individual education plans (IEPs) or options within digital learning to meet these students' needs. Thus, the extent to which digital learning enhances the educational experiences of students with special education needs in more meaningful ways is dependent on teachers' experience and ability to match instruction to students' needs.[21] For example, one MPS teacher printed the transcripts of online videos and had students highlight them, while another found practice tests and worked with students outside the online system on content support. For teachers without special education experience or training, access to certified special education teachers or aides was critical. Providing accommodations can also be made easier through individual or small group instruction, such as those offered by one-on-one tutoring or integrated in the school day while other students work on technology-directed learning tasks. However, instructors also need to have reasonable class sizes and supports in place to facilitate those types of accommodations. One instructor who was concerned about his ability to support students at lower reading levels remarked, "We need smaller class sizes than we have; I think I could do it well with thirty-five. One class we saw was seventy-four students; ideally, we would have twenty-five to thirty students. We need more time for one-on-one interactions with the students."

Support for Students at Risk of Not Graduating

In the same way digital learning programs can fail to accommodate students with special education needs, such programs are rarely designed to meet the needs of students disengaged from the learning process.[22] One teacher explained how the online instructional program used in MPS high schools was valuable for students with self-regulation skills, who could take advantage of opportunities to review content or progress quickly, but that all students did not possess the prerequisite skills to do so: "For students who learn better in the online format, it is better. They can self-manage the options well, whether they need extra time, or if they want to speed up, etc. So many options to individualize it, which can be great for students who know what they need. But for some, it is too much to manage—they don't know how."

For those students who don't know how to self-manage, options such as personalized pacing—typically facilitated through technology-driven instruction—may actually limit their learning. Instructors in MPS lab-style credit-recovery classrooms frequently expressed concern about students who were reading at or below the sixth-grade level, when the program was designed for students reading at a middle school level or higher. Some teachers sought to provide additional instructional support through one-to-one interactions with these students and the creation of supplemental resources when the classroom environment and student-teacher ratios enabled these efforts.

Some technology-based programs also offer tools that can assist teachers in identifying where and how best to meet these students' unique needs. In classes where technology drives instruction, data collected through digital tools has the potential to allow for more efficient identification and targeting of instructional supports. For instance, we observed some teachers using LanSchool, a classroom management software that allowed them to log into any of the students' accounts and see a screenshot of their desktops at that moment. A handful of teachers also used this feature to provide instructional support to students who were struggling with course content, while others used it to monitor student progress and identify students in need of more intensive, face-to-face support. To fully leverage digital learning-based resources, teachers need the skills and training, as well as adequate incentives and motivation, to utilize such features in ways that benefit student learning.

Students and teachers also commented on positive transformations in student orientations to learning, encouraged through the development of supportive student-teacher relationships as discussed in the "Redefining the Student-Teacher Relationship" section above. Integrated with intensive teacher involvement and smaller class sizes to foster a sense of belonging—along with opportunities to demonstrate competency through shorter, scaffolded modules—digital learning can be one part of the solution to re-engage students at risk of school failure.[23] However, in an unsupportive or disconnected learning environment, isolation and the increased emphasis on self-directed learning may have the opposite result, decreasing confidence and contributing to disengagement over time.[24] As the following excerpt from an observation of online instruction in a lab-style classroom shows, it depends largely on the role and efforts of the teacher:

> The student was at his desk, where a lesson on Chinese characters was playing. However, he did not use the headphones as the lecture played. Within a couple of minutes, the student got up. Nine minutes passed before the instructor noticed that the student was not at his desk, and he got up to find out if the student had checked out. The student returned but held his head in his hands and was looking down and not working. He started putting things in his backpack. He looked at a problem for a minute, but then got up from his desk again, while the video was still playing. Then he finished packing up and was leaving; he did not appear to take the time to log out and did not finish anything in the program.

In this example, there were two teachers in close proximity to the student, but their efforts to reengage him were minimal. Of course, classrooms are complicated places where many students come in with complex needs. Yet a loss of instructional time and opportunity is particularly concerning in contexts such as those we observed, where historically marginalized populations are disproportionately assigned to online learning labs.

Strategies to Build Instructor Capacity in Low-Resource Settings

The successful integration of digital tools in the classroom has the potential to transform learning for students, redefining the role of the teacher in ways that facilitate more individualized attention to student needs and that engage students in new, technology-enhanced modes of learning. As we have also shown in this chapter, however, in the absence of adequate training and the environmental conditions and supports essential for effective technology integration, these efforts can worsen inequities in student access to quality instructional experiences and learning opportunities.

We conclude by offering the following recommendations to increase the prospects for success in classroom technology integration:

- Take into account *teacher experience and instructional expertise as well as technical competency* when assigning teachers to classrooms integrating digital learning.
- *Build instructor capacity* to integrate technology for specific instructional goals and to customize its use for meeting distinct student needs; where possible, draw on *teacher peer assistance and mentoring* in expanding capacities for integrating digital learning.
- Provide teachers with *resources and training to use the real-time data collected through digital tools* to help focus student-teacher interactions, such as those around goal setting.
- *Reduce class sizes* to allow teachers to better facilitate blending learning and individualized instruction and to encourage higher rates of digital citizenship and extend support to all students within a classroom.
- Provide teachers with tools and supports to develop *professional relationships with students* that foster a sense of belonging and encourage students to engage in learning.
- Establish benchmarks and strategies *to identify and reassign students who may not be best served by technology-based instruction* to programs that provide more intensive, face-to-face teacher support.
- Develop a structure and resources for instructors to *ensure equitable student access* to resources and instructional supports for out-of-school learning.

Effective integration of digital learning initiatives at classrooms levels can be done neither on the cheap nor on the fly. Without the right levels of investment in the types of instructional—and infrastructure—supports proposed above, educators and administrators may need to reevaluate strategies that target academically marginalized students for the use of digital learning to avoid exacerbating educational inequities. However, by learning from the challenges teachers in our partnering districts faced and the solutions they developed through years of trial and error, as well as guidance from research, subsequent initiatives around digital learning can be designed and enacted in a manner more conducive to ensuring equity, while simultaneously expanding the quality of educational opportunities available to students in low-resource educational settings.

4

Ensuring Access to Quality Learning for Historically Marginalized Students

THE TERM *digital divide* once characterized disparate access to educational technology simply as: *Can you get online or access to a device with educational resources or not?* Recent telecommunications and technology advances have nearly eliminated this *first digital divide*, leading to a greater focus on equity in access to opportunities for skills-building (the *second digital divide*).[1] In fact, in the 2018–2019 school year, school districts across the US were using more than seven thousand different digital tools, with those designed to provide access to educational content seeing the greatest growth in use.[2] Students directed to digital learning may use these tools to acquire a range of skills, including: (1) basic *operational skills* for accessing digital resources and the internet, (2) *navigation skills* that enable students to effectively find, use, and evaluate the available information and digital resources, (3) *creative skills* for developing their own content and collaborating and sharing it with others, and (4) *social skills* for communicating and interacting in digital learning settings in ways that foster relationships and learning exchange.[3] In this chapter, we look in greater depth at how students are interacting with digital resources and engaging with others in educational contexts, with an eye toward identifying strategies to reduce disparities in their use and the skills developed by students of differing racial backgrounds, socioeconomic status, and levels of academic readiness. We also illuminate what researchers describe as the *third digital divide*—or the outcomes of digital learning.

Proponents of digital learning initiatives frequently highlight their potential to increase both student engagement in learning and their academic success by leveraging the novelty of learning with technology and the opportunity for students to get into the "driver's seat" and steer their use of digital programming according to their own educational interests and needs.[4] When technology facilitates opportunities for students to manipulate their learning environment, it also encourages higher-order thinking.[5] That said, in educational environments fixated on test scores, the goal to boost student engagement can sometimes seem like a secondary aim. A growing body of research, including work we describe in this chapter, suggests that in fact the two goals are closely intertwined—rates of learning are higher when students are more engaged.[6]

How do we observe the role of student engagement in the digital learning process? Conceptually, measures of student engagement seek to capture the extent to which students are psychologically invested in learning; in the classroom, we expect to see engaged students demonstrating greater effort, persistence, concentration, and enthusiasm for learning than disengaged students.[7] Moreover, engagement also embodies socioemotional dimensions, with active engagement more likely than passive engagement to inspire a passion for learning and sense of belonging, or social connectedness, in the learning environment. We have seen the full spectrum of student engagement levels across the different types of digital learning initiatives and educational settings where we have studied them, as well as within classroom environments. Indeed, while increased student engagement may often be assumed by technology designers and vendors to follow in lockstep with the delivery of digital tools to educational settings, our research and that of others suggests that this relationship is far from guaranteed. We begin below by describing how students are either directed to or provided opportunities to engage in digital learning, as well as how the resulting context for learning can influence their levels of engagement and digital citizenship.

The Intended Beneficiaries of Digital Learning and Their Learning Environments

As previously described, students who are directed to or provided opportunities to engage in digital learning in the large, urban school districts we studied tended to be from low-income settings, students of color (specifically Black or Hispanic) and, in many cases, falling behind their peers in academic attainment (as measured by test score performance or credit accumulation). Many students need access to *additional* supports to succeed academically, including those that might be facilitated through blended and personalized instructional models of learning with digital tools. As a matter of fact, the online tutoring program offered by Milwaukee Public Schools was intended to deliver exactly these types of supports by connecting students with opportunities to interact synchronously and individually (or in pairs) with an instructor who could offer more targeted assistance than feasible in the traditional, day-school classroom setting. And although one-to-one student-teacher interactions around digital learning were less readily facilitated in the Dallas Independent School District classrooms that received 1:1 tablets or the MPS online learning lab-style classrooms, in each of these contexts, the instructors could implement instructional formats that allowed for smaller group or one-to-one learning sessions, as described in chapter 3.

In considering the ways that the targeting of digital learning initiatives might create barriers to or opportunities for increasing student engagement in learning, we begin with the MPS online tutoring program. This program, which targets students falling behind academically, was straightforward in its aim to promote more intensive, 1:1 or 1:2 instructor-student interactions in a (potentially) more relaxed home setting. The primary benefit of this tutoring program was that targeted students received increased instructional time, which translated into positive achievement gains when students received at least forty hours of tutoring a year.

However, it was also not uncommon for students to have limited internet or phone bandwidth, sometimes from having to share with other household members during tutoring sessions. Such limitations, often disproportionately felt by students in low-resource settings, hampered teacher-student interactions. For instance, in the following example, we observed the teacher's audio cutting in and out, making it difficult for the student to hear directions or feedback.

STUDENT: "Are you there still?" [Teacher is cutting out again.]

TEACHER: "Do you see where I typed your name?" [Teacher is still cutting out.]

STUDENT: "Hello?" [Yells to mom again that her voice is skipping. Mom yells something back.]

The teacher asks if her cousin is still on the computer: "Is your cousin still online next to you? I am wondering if he is still too close."

The student yells for mom to move him because he is still too close. [The teacher explains that she thinks the computers are too close, not the people.] Mom yells she is coming.

TEACHER: "Leave the headphones unplugged so I can talk to her." The teacher says she is wondering if the computers are interfering with one another. She says she's sorry to bother her. Mom says it's fine. They are going to take her upstairs. She says she is doing a good job other than that, but she says her voice is skipping.

MOM: "It's hard to have two kids tutoring at the same time!"

Mom says she is thinking about shipping some of the things back because she doesn't think they are working.

Teacher thanks mom for help.

TEACHER: "Sometimes when two computers are together, they mess each other up."

In the above example, the instructor was able to work with the student and parent to resolve the access issue that was interfering with engagement in the lesson, but in other cases, instructors were not aware of or were unable to troubleshoot the kind of technical difficulties the student was experiencing. And in still other observed sessions, the instructor could not do anything about the distractions created by other family members who could be heard watching television or talking in the background. Such environmental constraints limited the time and opportunities for tutors to engage students in developing more creative digital learning skills, as well as the quality of the rapport instructors were able to build with the students.

However, it's important when evaluating a program such as this to consider the counterfactual. In other words, if students were *not* learning in this setting, what would their learning environment look like? In the case of tutoring, the alternative treatment would likely be unassisted studying or no studying at all. That helps to explain why despite the challenges, we found that one-on-one tutoring was still on average beneficial, particularly when students participated in forty or more hours a year.

In DISD, elementary schools with higher proportions of Hispanic students and ELLs were more likely to receive the 1:1 tablets: the proportion was 20 percent higher Hispanic (at 88 percent), and two-thirds were ELLs, compared with about half in other Title I schools. In these StEP initiative schools, we found that student engagement in digital learning increased with the intensity of tablet use and with blended instructional models, although as in the MPS tutoring program, student engagement declined with technology disruptions and low-rated learning environments. Importantly, we also found that ELLs were *more* engaged and benefited more from learning with the tablets, which challenges conventional beliefs that historically underserved populations will always face more barriers to engaging and learning with technology. Moreover, as discussed in chapter 3, if the students were learning with the tablets in *bilingual* classrooms, their level of engagement (measured in survey data and observations) was even higher, in part because teachers in bilingual classrooms were using blended instructional techniques approximately twice as often as teachers in traditional classrooms.[8]

In contrast, in the classrooms where MPS high school students were taking courses online, primarily after having failed a course in a traditional classroom setting, the use of blended or more personalized (one-to-one or small group) instructional strategies was a relatively rare occurrence. Large class sizes in these online learning environments limited instructor time and capacity for going beyond teaching basic operational or navigational skills to support more creative and engaging learning approaches. With educational content accessed asynchronously and with minimal interactions with live instructors, student engagement levels in these online learning environments (as rated in our observations) were generally low. They also provided few opportunities for students to foster relationships and learning exchange (or social skills) with their peers. One graduating student explained, for example, that she had taken courses online all four years of her high school career and regretted that she had missed out on opportunities for "hands-on" learning and meaningful discussions and interactions with her classmates. When teachers assumed primarily administrative roles (versus providing instructional or student support), which was predominant in these online credit-recovery classrooms, we saw student engagement and digital citizenship sag even further, with interactions between students primarily disruptive rather than constructive to learning.

This is another instance where describing the counterfactual may help to illuminate the role of digital tools in this environment. Notably, we saw a similar range of disruptions in traditional, face-to-face classroom observations conducted in the schools where students were enrolled in online courses at the highest rate. And despite low levels of attainment in the online courses, some students—particularly students who previously failed more courses and/or were previously chronically absent—came to school more often once they were assigned to online courses. This may have been because they benefited from the online course structure, which included short, modularized lessons with frequent opportunities for feedback. Additionally, there may have been benefits because the system also had a mechanism to provide more detailed feedback and adapt instruction to students' responses.

With digital tools currently flooding public schools and classrooms—the increase in the average number of products used in individual districts from the 2017–2018 to the 2018–2019 school year was 28 percent—it is imperative that we better understand how they can be used effectively to engage students creatively and socially in ways that reduce the *third digital divide*, or disparities in outcomes from their use. We now turn to examine in greater depth the various factors that promote or limit student engagement in digital learning.

Factors That Promote or Limit Student Engagement in Digital Learning

One notable reason that the acquisition and use of digitals tools is soaring and increasingly penetrating the instructional core in public schools is tight budgets. In the face of accountability pressures to increase student test scores and high school graduation rates with fewer resources in instructional budgets, digital tools have the potential to increase access to instructional time both during and outside the school day, at far less expense than hiring more teachers and tutors. For example, in reference to online course-taking used for credit recovery in high schools, the International Association for K–12 Online Learning described these programs as "low-cost," with "very low levels (if any) of teacher involvement," and that they "require very little of students in demonstrating proficiency."[9] Yet state and local educational administrators authorizing their purchase and use have argued, as former Texas Education Commissioner put it that "any tool that helps get kids credit toward graduation is certainly worth having."[10] Los Angeles Unified's Chief Academic Officer Frances Gipson claimed, "Whether it's online or any other credit-recovery course, it's the same."[11] In effect, with their expanding use, digital tools are changing the way school districts allocate resources, as well as how classrooms are organized and managed.

Classroom Organization and Management

Contrary to the perspectives of the educational administrators cited above, an unassailable finding in our research is that digital tools are not a cheap substitute for live instructor time in engaging students in learning. Yet classrooms are sometimes physically organized as if this were the case. For example, instructor-student interactions were not only constrained by high student-teacher ratios in many MPS class-rooms used for online course-taking, but the design or layout of the instructional space and positioning of the teacher in these classrooms also mattered noticeably for their engagement. In classrooms environments where the teacher sat at the front and students worked behind desktops in rows, there was little opportunity for fluid or impromptu communication between teachers and students. Students were often aware that the teacher could not see their screens (in the absence of a tool for local area network, or LAN, monitoring), and many took advantage of this to disengage from their courses and surf online, download music, watch sports, and more. Students could also readily anticipate a teacher's approach (e.g., when a teacher circled the classroom to check on students), and were quick to click on the program window that brought them back to the online course. In classrooms where teachers used LanSchool to monitor individual student screens, students sometimes stayed in the online program while instructional videos played, but with their headphones plugged into their cell phones to access non-educational content. Still, although we only saw LanSchool used in 10 percent of our whole-class observations in MPS, we found statistically significant, positive associations between teachers' computer-based monitoring of students and ratings of their engagement and interactions with students.

Indeed, digital tools such as the LanSchool system can be particularly helpful when students are working individually or on different tasks in online courses in a classroom. However, the effectiveness of teachers' use of these and similar systems can vary. In a classroom with three instructors, we observed one instructor who stayed at the front desk monitoring students via LAN technology, one who walked around checking on students, and one who worked one-on-one with a student who needed assistance. Unlike the modal observation, where a majority of students would disengage from their online courses as time passed, around thirty three of the thirty-five students in that classroom were working at any given time throughout the class period.

In this example, use of LAN technology was part of a comprehensive and *complimentary* support structure that encouraged students to stay on-task as one part of a larger instructional support system. It also facilitated some one-to-one teacher-student interactions. The result was one of the highest rates of student engagement in learning tasks that we observed in lab-style online course-taking classrooms. In contrast, the following example demonstrates the limitations and potential dehumanizing effect of a monitoring system when it is used *instead* of ongoing personal interaction with students:

> The teacher stayed in one place at a desktop at the back of the room; she did not move around the classroom to check students' work. A student yelled out, "I failed again; I need another [attempt]"; the teacher just said "OK" from the back of the room, and some of the other students laughed. Students were becoming less engaged in their work; only about half were working on their courses, and most of the others were on their cell phones. Students were not taking notes or working out problems. The instructor continued to stay at the back of the room and respond to students as needed.

As this example above suggests, insufficient instructor engagement in combination with only using technology for monitoring may exacerbate instead of mitigate factors contributing to low learner engagement or inequitable access to teachers, particularly for students less prepared to engage with digital tools.

We also observed styles or strategies for organizing and managing classrooms in both MPS and DISD that were more conducive to teacher-student interactions and student engagement. For example, some online course-taking classrooms in MPS were furnished with flexible seating in personalized learning initiatives (e.g., sofas, comfortable chairs, and/or round tables, along with laptop computers), which gave students different places from which to access their online courses. These more open or accessible spaces made it easier for teachers to monitor student activity and approach those who were lagging, and they also appeared to open opportunities for teachers to interact one-to-one with those who were struggling. At the same time, even the placement of the sofas relative to the positioning of the instructor could matter. In one classroom that included several tables and sofas, students could pick up their

Chromebooks and decide where they wanted to work. We observed only six students in the classroom during this period. Most of them chose to work from one of two sofas. The back of one sofa faced the front of the room, so it was harder to monitor the students sitting there. There was one main instructor and an aide at the front of the room. They did not go over to see what the students were doing at any time, but the instructors called out to the students several times to try to keep them on task in their work. The instructors' choice in this case to assume a more administrative rather than hands-on instructional role in managing the classroom and supporting student learning appeared to have an important effect on student engagement. Only one of the six students was observed to work consistently through most of the period, and by the last fifteen minutes, all the students had "checked out" and were no longer working on their courses. These cases reinforce the importance of structuring the classroom environment in a manner that demonstrates to students that despite the nontraditional format, they are still expected to engage in learning.

In DISD elementary classrooms, teachers would at times invite students to sit on a rug in the classroom, which created a space that was more relaxed and conducive to both teacher-student and peer-to-peer interactions as they worked on educational applications on the tablets. For example, it was easier for students to lean over and see each other's devices and collaborate on the activity at hand. This also made apparent one of the advantages of the 1:1 tablets over the 1:1 laptops that DISD initially rolled out—the tablets were easier for students to move with and manipulate (given their size in small hands), which teachers confirmed in interviews. DISD teachers also sometimes arranged students in circles or semicircles to facilitate collaboration in their work with the tablets, as well as to carve out time for personalized one-to-one instruction, as this excerpt from an observation illustrates:

> In one observation highly rated for student engagement, instructor engagement, and student-instructor interactions around the technology, students worked in groups on Kindles using a math application to complete an assignment. The instructor simultaneously worked with rotating groups of four students at a half-circle table at the back of the class-

room. She was constantly engaged, giving students one-to-one attention to walk them through the assignment, which included multiplication, division, and fractions. The students then went to work individually, while a few continued to work one-to-one with the instructor. They settled in and were on task working diligently on both their book and Kindle math assignments. When students had completed the problems assigned in the first math application, they were allowed to log into and complete personalized math learning activities on the Kindles. This second program provided live support from a certified, bilingual teacher and integrated a "motivational system" to encourage student interest. About thirty minutes into the period, the instructor switched to a recap of the lesson and an informal assessment of how students felt about their progress on the lesson. She also went through a recap of definitions from the lesson, concretely defining them for students and having students define them for each other. Even with eighteen students in the classroom, the teacher managed to organize the classroom and her time with students to give every student an opportunity for one-to-one, personalized instruction. The lesson also reflected an example of high-quality blended instruction, as the teacher integrated live instruction with self-directed or cooperative tablet use in varying ways that also enabled her to assess how well students were grasping the content.

Finally, perhaps one of the clearest advantages of digital tools in regard to classroom organization and management is the option they may create for "anytime, anywhere" access to digital learning experiences. In DISD, the district chose not to allow students to take tablets home, largely because of concerns for their maintenance and security. But in MPS, elementary students and their parents could arrange tutoring sessions online at their convenience, and high school students had log-in IDs that enabled them to access and work on their online courses from any place that they could get internet access on a device. Using data from the online course program vendor that allowed us to identify the time of day of each student log-in and activities in their online courses while logged into the system, we were able to generate categories or profiles of student users. Among them was a group that we labeled the "moonlighters," because of their frequent use of the online course-taking program outside of the school day. The moonlighters were one of two student user types that we characterized as more engaged users—they were less often idle in their online courses, completed more activities with less session time, and completed their courses in fewer sessions. However, we also found that the students who took advantage of the opportunity to work on their courses outside of school were less likely to be economically disadvantaged or to have special educational needs, and they also had the strongest prior-year academic performance of the four user types we identified. We surmise that this reflects in part disparate access to the resources or supports necessary to engage in online courses in out-of-school settings, including unequal access to devices, high-speed internet, or someone to offer instructional or technical assistance outside of school hours.

We heard from a number of teachers who, recognizing the value of extending student learning outside the school day for *all* of their students, recounted exceptional efforts to overcome student barriers to engaging in online instruction outside of their classrooms. One teacher described opening emails from kids until 9:00 p.m.—and often much later—to unlock or help them progress through a course. He showed us an email from 12:30 a.m. the previous night, saying, "If kids are motivated enough to work at home, the least I can do is respond." Another teacher explained how he recognized and accommodated student needs for different options for digital learning during and after school hours: "I try integrating more digital applications into teaching in the classroom. I set kids up to work with another program on the weekend. Everyone learns differently, so I want to make sure I have different options for them. I bring that in, I have set this up as an app on my phone so that I can send them things over the weekend. I do this with YouTube videos; I bring them everything I can."

Clearly, this type of supplemental help from teachers wouldn't be possible without the integration of technology in their classrooms. While not feasible for all teachers, providing student access to support outside the school days not only incentivizes out-of-school learning, but it also demonstrates a personal commitment to students' success. That said, if teachers are expected to be accessible to students outside school hours or to fulfill responsibilities that go beyond the traditionally defined teacher role, this should be explicitly stated, compensated for, and supported through training to ensure interactions are beneficial to students and do not put undue strain on teachers. Again, digital tools should not be a substitute for school district investments in instructor time, capacity, and support.

Curricular Content

The increasing private-sector penetration of the public school market for digital learning has accelerated in recent years, extending into the "technical core" or work processes of public education—that is, to the provision of curricular content and wholesale delivery of core course instruction in public schools. The curriculum delivered through online and digital software is most often vendor-developed.[12] For-profit vendors may prioritize efficiency through standardization of content over curricula that adapt to local contexts and student needs. Furthermore, standardized course content can be more readily scaled than curricula that are truly culturally responsive, making it increasingly profitable for vendors and cost-effective for school districts. These market incentives run contrary, however, to what we have learned about the types of instructional materials that increase student engagement and persistence in learning—that is, content that resonates with students' lived realities, interests, and learning needs.[13] This incongruence also raises concern for how students who fall outside of the normative grade-level expectations that guide the software developers, such as those who have already been marginalized in traditional educational settings, will respond to vendor-developed content that is less likely to reflect their day-to-day realities.

Indeed, given the advent of the Common Core State Standards and the recent attention to core content learning and its influence on how instructional materials are used in the classroom, there has been surprisingly little acknowledgment that a growing proportion of public school students are getting curriculum content, and often its delivery, through private vendors whose materials, while meeting the letter of the regulation, may fail to support the student experiences CCSS was designed to facilitate. Recognizing this, we studied an online course-taking system used by MPS to better understand the curricular content and instructional techniques employed in online courses, particularly in regard to understanding the extent to which the online course content was culturally relevant and responsive.

Alignment to state standards is important, but even more important to student engagement is whether the online coursework is aligned and responsive to students' lived experiences, including their cultural contexts. For example, making certain instructional content available in students' home language is key. We found that the online courses offered written translations of the instruction accessible in languages such as Spanish and French, but the students who needed translations in languages such as Burmese, Somali, Arabic, or Hindi (more common in the district population) did not receive similar accommodation. In addition, as a function of the standardized structure of the courses, the remote instructors communicated the same expectations for academic progression to all students, which rarely reflected high academic standards or responsiveness to students' needs or cultural backgrounds. High school credit-recovery courses, which we observed in the classrooms as well, did not facilitate group work or collaboration among the students, which precluded the development of a sense of community and social skills among the online learners. The courses were also not designed to capture information on students' personal learning preferences, their home lives, or cultural backgrounds and thereby could not adapt the course content or structure based on this information if it were to be collected. Instead, any adaptations to students' needs, interests, or cultural context had to be facilitated by a live instructor within a blended learning context, which, as we discussed in chapter 3, was rarely observed in practice.

These insights are consistent with prior research, which has shown that the cultural background, concerns, and informational needs of students of color are rarely prioritized by content providers, which can contribute to a decreased sense of belonging, learned helplessness, stereotype threat, and internalized oppression.[14] Although our study did capture a few promising examples of courses weaving in more diverse content representative of the student populations they served, online course modules also provided some examples of troubling and problematic representations of historically marginalized students.

For example, the following excerpt from our field notes exemplifies how digital learning tools can further marginalize students of color through the very content of the course:

> When talking about the Constitutional Convention, the teacher said, "The convention was a gathering of great men. Thomas Jefferson called them 'a gathering of demigods.'" The instructor then repeated this at the wrap-up of the section with no context or counter-narrative of how many of these same "demigods" also owned slaves and actively argued to keep certain rights (voting, owning property, running for office) from entire groups of people based on their race, gender, or class. The instructor referred to Washington numerous times as the "Father of the United States" and Madison as the "Father of the Constitution." While talking about the Connecticut Compromise, there was a bullet on "number of members based on free inhabitants plus 3/5 of the slave population," which was described in mechanical terms of how the math would work, but not in terms of the ethical and moral decisions/implications this compromise represented. At the end, the instructor asked [paraphrased]: "How would your own lives be changed if the compromises hadn't of happened, including would we still have slavery?" Then he just left it at that, which could perpetuate trauma for those students whose ancestors were enslaved. In the same lesson, the example of Missouri Compromise was invoked. The instructor said it contributed to peace for a while, without any discussion of for whom the Missouri Compromise brought peace and for whom it did not.

Although these issues certainly are present in traditional classroom settings as well, the limited ability to adapt the online course content or instructional tasks to the local study body and classroom environment may worsen these consequences in digital learning, particularly for the types of students whom we have seen directed to digital learning (e.g., with prior course failures or other academic challenges). Compounding these concerns, we also frequently saw student engagement and attendance diminish with their time in the online learning labs, and other research evidence likewise shows that students who struggle to achieve success in their online courses exhibit decreasing motivation and increasing alienation over time.[15]

Alternatively, one benefit of the often-standardized nature of digital-based learning is that efforts toward making curricular content more culturally competent and relevant are often easier to scale. We believe there is an opportunity for vendors, educators, and researchers to partner in leveraging digital tools in this manner. In fact, our research continues in partnership with MPS and a vendor of online courses, in which we are engaging in a process of reviewing and redesigning online course content. We see potential for this and similar collaborations among school districts, ed-tech vendors, and researchers to improve the quality and cultural relevance of online educational content and structures.

Instructional Strategies

In response to potential inadequacies in online curricula, such as those described above—which may be exacerbated in but are not limited to online courses—classroom teachers can employ various evidence-based strategies to increase access to quality educational experiences and engagement for students from historically marginalized groups.[16] For example, to prepare students to develop cultural competence and a critical consciousness that aids them in succeeding academically, teachers can help them to build the requisite knowledge, skills, and behaviors on a base of mutual respect and effective communication. The idea is for students to learn how to traverse both community and dominant cultural norms, with the understanding that a particular set of attitudes, preferences, and behaviors may lead to more favorable outcomes in a specific setting, but without attaching greater general value to one culture over another.[17] For instance, one way for teachers to do this is to incorporate more critical analysis of course content relevant to students' lives into classroom learning, while encouraging students to assume an active role in discussions that promote understanding of race and culture.[18] The more teachers interact with and strive to foster communication that promotes cultural understanding and responsiveness, the more effective they will be in adapting their instructional delivery to student needs and drawing students into more creative and productive uses of digital tools for learning.

More generally, it is clear that technology deployed in classrooms without transformative pedagogy will do little to enhance student learning, as highlighted in chapter 3. In DISD, for example, we used data from teacher professional development sessions (e.g., lessons that teachers prepared based on their professional development) to characterize teacher knowledge and preparation for integrating digital tools into their classroom. The teachers who were least experienced or prepared for this work developed plans for incorporating technology into their instruction that reflected no substantive modifications to their teaching philosophies. For instance, a teacher might substitute an application on the tablets for worksheets used for test preparation if the teacher viewed tablets as a means to individualize test practice, including the pace or level. In such cases, neither the instructor nor the students benefited from the capabilities of digital tools to facilitate student-centered, collaborative, active, and critical thinking-based learning.[19] We found that students were, on average, 40 percent more likely to be engaged in classrooms that offered blended learning with the tablets; that is, the instruction combined teacher and technology-directed tasks in creative ways. However, at least initially, the district's capacity for customizing the teacher professional development sessions was limited, so that those with less ease and experience could be provided more support to acquire these types of technology integration skills. Over time, in partnership with the Jiv Daya Foundation, DISD expanded teacher PD at both the start of the school year and throughout the year, and it also shifted the distribution of tablets to "feeder pattern schools" to facilitate more teacher peer-to-peer collaborations in capacity-building for creative uses of the tablets.

With the ever-expanding capabilities of digital tools and the higher levels of competency they require for fully utilizing their features, it will be critical for state and local agencies, as well as vendors, to consider the assumptions highlighted in chapter 2. For example, districts should set aside more resources for increasing staff and instructor knowledge of effective technology applications and websites, as well as for ongoing professional learning opportunities on how to leverage those capabilities. In some states and districts, it may also be essential to increase resources for hiring more certified teachers. We observed more favorable rates of instructor engagement, interactions with the students and technology, and student engagement, as well as improved physical environments for learning, in classrooms where students had access to one or more certified teachers. Yet we also found a higher proportion of substitute teachers serving as instructors in online credit-recovery classrooms. The presence of a substitute teacher, whether long-term or single-day, in a credit-recovery classroom was significantly associated with less favorable ratings of instructor engagement.[20] Ratings of instructor-student digital tool interactions were also significantly lower in classrooms with a substitute teacher. In one class, an observer noted that the "students weren't accessing the software during the session, primarily because it was a sub that day who didn't have access to the program and couldn't help." In another observation, a substitute teacher refrained from monitoring student engagement to prevent "starting something," communicating low expectations in the process. And in a more extreme case, the substitute teacher "did not play an active role, and at some point, just left the classroom." These instances illustrate common challenges in low-resource districts related to staffing shortages, but also highlight the disservice done to students who, in the absence of a teacher with even limited capabilities to support their use of digital tools, are effectively deserted in the learning process.

Strategies to Improve Student Engagement in Low-Resource Settings

Drawing on our findings, we present the following recommended strategies for district and school leaders and staff to improve student engagement in digital learning, particularly in the context of classrooms serving historically marginalized students:

- Select digital learning-based tools and programs that *facilitate the options and accommodations for customization* that meet the needs of your student population.

- Use your *leverage as customers to pressure vendors* into demonstrating (before a contract is signed) the ways in which they ensure cultural awareness, competence, relevance, and responsiveness in their instructional materials, and embed this in the contract.
- Consider the *role of youth and family voice in your decision making* and review processes.
- Set clear expectations and increase resources and support for *the integration of blended learning techniques* that leverage the benefits of both face-to-face and technology-based learning.
- Carefully deliberate and continually reassess which students are assigned to what types of digital learning opportunities to *ensure alignment between program features and students' educational needs.*
- Implement a process to regularly evaluate the extent to which digital learning tools *in practice* and the resources allocated to support their integration are adequately meeting the educational needs of students.
- *Provide additional support or reassign students* to a better-aligned learning environment to facilitate student success as needed.
- Work with vendors of digital tools to *design better courses and applications*, with an eye toward making them more responsive to the cultures, contexts, and lived experiences of the students they serve and increasing student engagement.
- Demand that external curricular reviews *involve individuals who are diverse and representative of the student populations you serve.* Consider bringing student representatives onto review panels who also are compensated as experts in their own lived experiences and learning needs.
- Explore what training your administration and staff need in order to *be more culturally responsive to the communities you serve* with your products.

For *school-based educators* who are implementing digital learning on the ground and in classrooms and who typically facilitate, manage, supplement, or provide the scaffolding around ed-tech integration, we suggest:

- Know the digital content and tools and ask for demo access so you can *see what the content looks like* before adopting or implementing it in your class.
- *Ask your students* what they think of the digital content.
- *Critically reflect* on the content component of the pedagogic approach that is created by the vendor.
- Look for leverage points in the digital platform or device where you can *inject your own content, assignments,* and other supplementary materials.
- Leverage other teachers in your district who are working with the same digital content or tools and *create a shared space* (e.g., a collaborative online folder) where people can upload supplementary/support materials, as well as professional development opportunities created by teachers experienced in using digital tools.
- *Communicate to the district* the specific types of training you feel you need in order to maximize any supplementary materials and critical reflection with students.

Lastly, even though they are the end-users with potentially the most at stake in digital learning initiatives, students rarely have a voice in the processes of developing, choosing and evaluating the effectiveness of digital tools. Advocacy is needed at all levels in the educational system, but particularly at district and school levels, to ensure that the best interests of students are factored into all aspects of the adoption and implementation of digital learning. Particularly when student engagement is the goal, students cannot be passive participants in their educational journey.

5

Changing
Achievement Trajectories
with Digital Learning

THE 2001 ELEMENTARY AND SECONDARY EDUCATION ACT (No Child Left Behind) was introduced as one of the federal government's most sweeping efforts to close achievement gaps between economically disadvantaged and minoritized students and their peers. The NCLB mandate for schools to administer annual testing in grades 3–8, with results reported by poverty, race/ethnicity, and limited English proficiency, transformed K–12 education with an accountability system laser-focused on student performance (as measured on state standardized tests). One of NCLB's less widely recognized goals was the promotion of educational technology integration across all grades and core subjects in K–12 education, including reading, mathematics, and science, as well as special education.[1] This translated into the expectation that all students would become "literate" in technology use: technology would be used to enhance instructional approaches in the classroom, and technology would be effectively integrated into the instruction provided to students. In effect, educational technology integration was a central element of the NCLB reforms that were launched to improve student academic achievement and overcome disparities in access to quality learning opportunities and in student educational outcomes.

In this chapter, we focus on whether the use of digital tools affects students' educational outcomes. In particular, drawing on the rigorous research evidence we co-generated in our two study districts, we explore in-depth how student access to and engagement in digital learning—at different ages and grades over time, as well as in differing environments—affects students' educational progress. As we noted in chapter 4, there are now more than seven thousand different digital tools in use in school districts across the country, and insights from research on digital learning are particular to the contexts in which they are studied, including tools used, grade level, student populations. We examine how three widely used types of digital tools affect student learning opportunities and outcomes spanning elementary through high school levels. In particular, we examine how student use of tablets in elementary school affects their performance in school; the extent to which students benefit from online course-taking in high school, and whether out-of-school tutoring through online platforms helps to improve student outcomes.

We relate these findings to concerns about equity in access to and implementation of digital learning, identifying student subgroups who may be left behind (or better assisted) in their educational progress and examples of policy and programmatic changes that could be made to prevent these students from losing additional ground in digital learning.

Factors That Influence Student Outcomes Through Digital Learning

We begin with a conceptual model (figure 5.1) that illustrates how various factors in educational settings could support or constrain student learning through their use of educational technology. For example, in chapter 2, we saw that it is often assumed that schools will have internet access with full capacity to support classroom connectivity needs in the rollout of digital learning initiatives. However, this is not always true in practice. As shown in the model, teachers' prior experience with technology and the level of support they receive on campus for troubleshoot-

Figure 5.1

Conceptual model of factors supporting or limiting outcomes

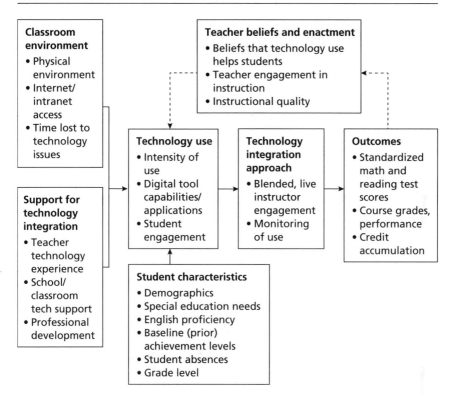

ing technology issues can, in turn, affect the time available for student use and for live teacher interactions in supporting student learning with technology. The pathway whereby teacher beliefs about the potential for educational technology to transform learning (see chapter 3) may also influence the extent to which they invest in integrating technology in their classrooms. Accordingly, professional development that supports technology use and integration in the classroom and contributes to its effectiveness in increasing learning can create a feedback loop through which improvements in student outcomes reinforce teacher beliefs that digital learning helps students. Finally, in chapter 4, we explored how students engage with educational technology and the student characteristics that are correlated with the intensity with which they use digital tools—for instance, our finding that economically disadvantaged students and those with special educational needs were less likely to work on and make progress in their online courses outside the school day. In this chapter, we describe how these factors, as depicted in figure 5.1, come together in the implementation of digital learning to influence students' educational outcomes.

Digital Learning Outcomes Among Elementary School Students

For nearly two decades, a core educational goal—articulated in law and pursued across state, district, school, and classroom levels—has been to increase student achievement through digital learning. Educational technology initiatives have also increasingly been seen as a means to reduce racial and socioeconomic gaps in student achievement. It is thus critical to examine their outcomes and effectiveness in settings where these gaps are particularly glaring.

To examine this at the elementary school level, we immersed ourselves in the Dallas Independent School District, an urban district that serves a predominately low-income, Hispanic student population, including many students whose first language is not English. As described in chapter 1, DISD launched a districtwide technology pilot initiative focusing on under-resourced K–12 classrooms, beginning with 1:1 laptops across all grade levels and then switching to primarily tablets for students in third- to fifth-grade classrooms. The 1:1 tablet distribution was characterized as a "personalized learning" initiative and by design served a significantly higher proportion of students who were Hispanic (88 percent, or 20 percent more than non-participating schools) and a significantly larger fraction of students with limited English proficiency (64 percent versus about 50 percent in non-participating schools).

We sought to understand the extent to which the tablet integration was associated with improved student outcomes, particularly reading and math test scores and student engagement. To this end, we conducted classroom observations of tablet use in six of the DISD elementary schools, then linked the data collected in classroom observations to teacher and student surveys and administrative data that included detailed student records (including their standardized test scores). Per our conceptual model, we examined the associations between student outcomes (standardized math and reading test scores) and the type and intensity of tablet use in the schools, controlling for student engagement and other student characteristics (including their prior-year academic achievement), teacher beliefs about technology, technology expertise and use of blended instruction, and time lost to technology problems in the classroom.

Student Achievement and Factors Correlated with Outcomes

In DISD, tablet users achieved higher math and reading scores on the state standardized tests than students in classrooms without access to tablets. In particular, the average effects in math corresponded to reductions in the achievement gap for economically disadvantaged students of 47 percent in math and 62 percent in reading, benchmarked against the fourth grade National Assessment of Educational Progress scores.[2] As we expected, we also found that time lost in the classroom to technical problems with the tablets or internet reduced the gains experienced by students, as shown starkly in figure 5.2. When teachers and students lost more than 25–30 percent of classroom instructional time to troubleshooting technology problems, the gains from technology use were erased, with students potentially experiencing greater learning losses than if they had not used the technology at all. Furthermore, teachers' prior experience with technology was positively associated with their students' achievement outcomes, which also related to their capability for managing technical challenges in the classroom. For less experienced teachers, the availability of school-based technology specialists to provide timely assistance and/or peer support from other technology-savvy teachers in the same building can be crucial to minimizing disruption to planned lessons and learning losses.

One likely pathway to the reductions in student achievement gains associated with problems in accessing and using devices and programs in the classroom is the level of student engagement in digital lessons

Figure 5.2

Consequences of instructional time lost to technology problems

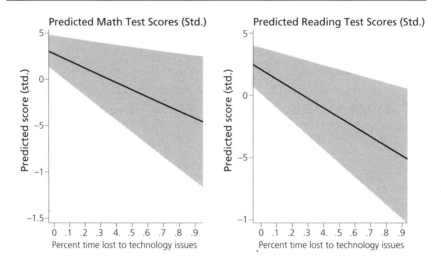

and learning (as shown in figure 5.1). For example, in DISD elementary school classes, when a teacher who is trying to launch a lesson needs to pause and walk around the room to troubleshoot log-in problems or find a program for a half dozen students, fifteen to twenty minutes (or a third of an instructional session) can easily disappear. And it is not unusual for students who are waiting for further instructions or the start of a blended lesson from a teacher to get distracted or to explore other uses for the device. As our analysis showed, because student engagement is positively associated with time or intensity of device use, and greater student engagement is in turn linked to increased student achievement, the loss of instructional time to technology problems is costly for student learning. Moreover, if technology challenges and teacher inexperience also limit the teacher's capacity for blending live instructional time with digital applications, student engagement and achievement may be further constrained. In fact, our analyses showed that students in classrooms where blended learning strategies were in use were 40 percent more likely to be engaged (on average) in learning.

One of the most effective ways to head off these potential barriers to the success of technology integration in schools and classrooms is to provide intensive professional development that boosts teacher technology knowledge and experience *at the start* of digital learning initiatives (see figure 5.1). In DISD elementary schools, students taught by a teacher with prior technology experience at the beginning of the year were 13 percent more likely to be engaged in digital learning, and increases in teacher technology experience over the school year were associated with an additional 15 percent increase in student engagement. We also found that teachers who rated themselves as expert technology users at the beginning of the school year used the tablets in the classroom more frequently, which, as discussed above, contributes to greater gains in student achievement as well.

Indeed, the teachers we interviewed in Dallas, even those with some previous technology experience, all wanted more professional development to prepare them for digital instruction, and they wanted additional or refresher trainings throughout the school year. As one teacher advised, "Do not assume that if one teacher knows, everyone knows. Trainers usually focus on the 'expert' teachers and forget about the ones who need to learn the basics." Another teacher explained why it would be helpful to have training at regular intervals rather than a flurry of sessions at the beginning of the school year: "The trainings were quick, and there was a lot of information to try to retain from them. Even after writing down the instructions and receiving flyers, it was overwhelming." Ongoing confidence- and skill-building for teachers can also contribute to the feedback loop shown in figure 5.1, in which teachers who believe that technology helps students to learn use the devices more and in blended instructional approaches, both of which increase student achievement. Not surprisingly, teachers in physical environments that were more accommodating to technology use were more likely to express favorable views of technology integration, and they lost less time to technical problems in the classroom. Even the most experienced teacher technology users will struggle to execute a lesson that relies on using an internet-based application when connectivity is failing or sporadic.

Encouragingly, students gained more in math achievement during the second year of the program for the same amount of tablet use. We observed more highly rated (instructor-facilitated) implementation of curricular content with the tablets and improved instructional models, including the creation of higher-quality learning opportunities through blended learning and student assessment with the tablets. In addition, students were more frequently using technology as intended. One of the strategies that DISD implemented in the second year to strengthen teacher capacity for effective technology use was a selective fellowship program that drew on the more knowledgeable and experienced teachers and provided them with time and resources to serve as peer leaders in supporting their colleagues. The district also intentionally shifted to a "feeder pattern" model of tablet distribution (i.e., introducing tablets to elementary schools that transitioned students into the same secondary schools), which facilitated more learning and sharing of effective technology integration practices across schools, such as tips for using particular applications or troubleshooting wireless access or device problems.

How Emergent Bilingual Elementary Students Benefit from Learning with Technology

Nearly a quarter of all elementary school students in the US speak a language other than English, with about 13 percent of kindergarten through sixth-grade students classified as English language learners.[3] As the number of students identified as ELL or bilingual in public schools continues to grow rapidly, increasing attention is being paid to the persistent achievement gaps between ELL and non-ELL students. In DISD, approximately one-half of all students were classified as ELL, and as noted above, closer to two-thirds of the students in the schools participating in the 1:1 technology initiative were identified as having limited English proficiency. Thus, DISD provided a pertinent educational setting in which to examine the potential for digital tools to support the learning of this fast-growing student population.

Educational technology, if implemented with sufficient teacher capacity and appropriate instructional strategies, can play a valuable role in mitigating achievement gaps and improving the underlying learning experiences that contribute to these gaps for ELL students in K–12 classrooms.[4] For example, digital programs and tools that facilitate deeper learning, provide opportunities for interactivity, and recognize the importance of the larger cultural context for language learning and literacy have been shown to accelerate language acquisition, while technology used for drill and practice is less likely to improve student learning.[5] Providing teachers with exposure to digital programs and tools aligned with best practices for teaching emergent bilingual students can also help them manage the greater variability in the utility of educational technology for this student population. It is especially important, for instance, to ensure that the programs used can be tailored to offer emergent bilingual students reading materials at their individually assessed reading level. It is often the case that teachers working in school districts with a high proportion of ELLs will be required to teach to a wider range of skill levels in their classrooms. To the extent that digital tools can better facilitate the adaptability of lessons to student language needs and thereby encourage and support their active learning, they may not only improve English language acquisition but also these students' overall academic performance in school.

In fact, ELL students in DISD who had access to tablets made larger gains in reading performance, particularly when they received at least forty minutes of weekly use in bilingual classrooms. In addition, these gains emerged more quickly for students in bilingual classrooms than in traditional classrooms, and they continued to rise with greater intensities of use. More specifically, the effects on student reading achievement for students in bilingual classrooms grew to more than double the size of the average reading effects for students in traditional classrooms when the devices were used for up to three hours a week in reading. We also more frequently observed teachers using blended instructional strategies in language instruction and found that these strategies were even more critical and effective for student learning in bilingual classes. As the use of blended learning strategies was associated with both teachers' technical and instructional capacities, strengthening their pedagogical expertise is as critical as building their confidence and skills in using the digital tools to facilitate student-centered instruction.

Digital Learning Outcomes Among High School Students

The pace of expansion of digital learning has been especially rapid at the high school level, where digital instruction usually takes place through use of programs that deliver course content online and allow "anywhere, anytime" access to courses required for graduation. Since NCLB-mandated reporting of graduation rates by states, online course-taking programs that increase options for credit recovery and accumulation have become a popular policy lever used by states to increase high school graduation. The Every Student Succeeds Act (ESSA) that replaced NCLB not only continues to include high school graduation rates as a key performance indicator in US educational accountability systems, but also imposes consequences for schools that fail to achieve a graduation rate of 67 percent. According to a 2014–2015 US Department of Education survey, nearly 90 percent of US high schools now offer at least one credit-recovery course, and online course-taking for credit recovery is expanding more rapidly in high-poverty, urban high schools. In MPS, nearly every high school in the district enrolled students in online courses in at least one year over the course of our study, and by 2016–2017, 40 percent of graduating seniors had completed at least one course through the online course-taking system.

Our deeper dive into what digital learning looks like in practice at the high school level and its implications for student academic and post–high school outcomes was motivated in large part by concerns about the potential for differential access to quality learning experiences for students directed to take their courses online. Our analyses showed that students taking courses online more frequently in high school were more likely to be Black, Hispanic, and ELLs; economically disadvantaged; and failing more courses and absent from school more often—in effect, separated in learning settings from their peers who were less likely to be falling behind academically. We saw this firsthand in MPS, where students interacted with an online instructional program that is used in school districts in all fifty states. We examined how the students engaged in online course-taking and the factors (as shown in figure 5.1) that impeded or supported their opportunities to learn and make academic progress in high school. For example, we assessed intensity of use not only by the number of online courses that students took, but also by the time they spent in a given online session, how many activities they were completing in a day, the ratio of idle to active time in sessions, and the percentage of sessions taking place outside the regular school day. We were able to link this information on students' online course interactions with their performance in their online courses and other measures of academic progression in high school, including credits earned, grade point average, and test score performance.

High School Student Educational Outcomes and Factors Correlated with Them

In chapters 3 and 4, we described the role of the instructor and the classroom environment in supporting technology integration; here we focus in greater depth on student-level interactions with the technology and how student characteristics interact with the other factors shown in figure 5.1 to influence their educational outcomes. For example, we were able to identify distinct patterns in student use of the online course-taking system that in turn influenced their course performance and other educational outcomes. Engaged student users—who spent more time working in a given course session (with less idle time) and completed more activities per day—were more likely to be eleventh- and twelfth-graders. These upper-level students made greater weekly progress toward course completion and accumulated course credits toward high school graduation at a faster rate than similar students who were not using the online course-taking system.[6]

Alternatively, ninth- and tenth-grade students were comparatively less productive users of the online course-taking system, spending close to half of their time in course sessions not interacting with the system (idle), fewer sessions interacting with their courses, and fewer activities in their courses per day than the more engaged upper-level students. Teachers pointed out that some of these students were simply unprepared for or incompatible with a fully online instructional system, sometimes entering at reading levels well below expectations for effective use of the system or with poorer self-regulation skills:

> Some of the underclassmen are in here all day and it is not working very well; underclassmen do not appreciate the opportunity of making up classes. They do not work . . . They are not at the reading level of the program.

> [Older students] aren't as distracted by phones, music, etc., because they (a) have been out there and are super motivated to graduate, and (b) are developmentally more ready to focus, just with their brains.

At the same time, as described in chapter 3, teachers in classrooms or online learning labs where the online instructional program was accessed were more likely to play an administrative role—getting students logged in, completing tasks like attendance counts, and monitoring students' use of their devices with a LAN system or occasional check-ins—rather than engaging in live or blended instruction that might help students to bridge gaps in their capabilities for effectively interacting with the system.

We accordingly found that for each additional percentage point of time spent idle in the course-taking system, online pass rates fell by about one-third of a percent and on-time pass rates by about one-fifth. This is relative to average course-passing rates of about 30 percent and on-time pass rates of about 17 percent in the online course-taking system across the time frame of our study. Online course grades (on a scale of 0 to 100) were about 0.42 points lower for each additional percentage point of time spent idle in an online session. So, for example, students with 10 percentage points more idle time in their course sessions would receive a course grade that was about 4.2 points lower, on average.

On a more positive note, we also found that course-taking behaviors associated with better online course outcomes were continually improving over time, as were the indicators of online course performance, including passing rates and on-time completion. In addition, the number of students accessing online course sessions outside the school day nearly doubled during the period of our study. We believe these patterns of improving online course outcomes likely reflected a combination of three plausible drivers. First, the school district encouraged schools to establish policies that promoted more efficient and effective student use of the online course-taking system, such as limiting the number of online courses students could initiate at any one time and requiring students to take notes while watching instructional videos in order to get approval to take an online quiz or test. Second, the instructors were asked to more closely monitor student progress in the online system, set goals with them, and to "disable" course access for students habitually falling behind, while younger students who appeared to be exerting low effort in the courses were largely discouraged from online course-taking. Thus, in part, these evolving patterns of use reflected changes in who was taking courses online over time. And third, there was a substantial increase in the proportion of students taking and passing course pre-tests—for example, with pre-test passing rates increasing from about one-quarter of students in 2013–2014 to about two-thirds in 2016–2017—which allowed students to "test out of" or bypass some or all parts of online course modules and thereby complete courses in fewer sessions. This latter potential explanation raises concerns about whether course passing rates imply mastery of content or learning that would be reflected in other measures of academic progress, such as student performance on standardized achievement tests.

When we examined associations between online course-taking and student achievement—comparing online course-takers to similar students who were failing courses and re-taking them in traditional classroom settings—we identified negative associations between online course-taking and math and reading test scores, as well as credits earned and GPAs at the end of the academic year. Comparisons between eleventh- and twelfth-graders and the ninth- and tenth-graders, however, showed that upper-level students were earning one-fifth to one-fourth more credits per year on average, and that replacing their failed credits with completed (online) course credits also raised their GPAs by as much as one-tenth of a point. That said, across grade levels, we continued to find negative associations between online course-taking and student standardized test scores, suggesting that online course-taking was generally not increasing student achievement—and some students may even have been set back in their learning. In fact, our analysis of the intensity of online course-taking showed that these associations became stronger (increasingly negative) with more years of online course-taking. We believe this finding raises serious concerns about equity in access to quality learning opportunities, given that this subgroup of academically struggling students—who were failing more courses and more likely to have been suspended—were more often being directed to online instructional environments that provided fewer supports for their learning.

Digital Learning and High School Graduation

Despite the dismal progress in raising student test scores through digital learning, some research has linked participation in online course-taking programs, primarily for credit recovery, to the dramatic uptick in graduation rates nationally. The most recently available graduation rate statistics (from January 2019) reported an adjusted cohort graduation rate (ACGR) for public high school students of 84.6 percent (for the 2016–2017 school year), the highest rate since it was first tracked in 2010–2011 (at 79 percent). However, as national statistics are not showing advances in student academic success on measures of high school student performance, such as the National Assessment of Educational Progress (NAEP) or the Programme for International Students Assessment (PISA), we are left again to question whether the online courses are adding value to students' learning, even if they help them to complete their degrees.[7]

The value of lifetime, gross economic benefits to the public associated with an additional high school graduate is estimated to be substantial, over $200,000 (in 2004 dollars). Another way that students might benefit from attaining their high school diploma through online course-taking, even if they do not learn the content as well, is that it provides them with a gateway credential for enrolling in postsecondary education programs. Of three million high school completers in 2015,

69 percent enrolled in college by the following October, which, according to NCES, represents an increase in the immediate college enrollment rate of six percentage points since 2000.[8] At the same time, if online course-taking in high school substitutes lower-quality digital instruction for better-quality live instruction, student learning at the postsecondary level could be hampered by weaker preparation for college-level coursework and for types of learning (e.g., group or hands-on) that may be expected at the college level. We therefore examined, first, whether online course-taking increased high school graduation rates in MPS, and second, whether online course-taking in high school was associated with increased college enrollment; we also looked at institutional quality where these students enrolled.

Looking at raw numbers, we saw that high school graduation and college enrollment rates were significantly higher for high school students with no online course-taking versus *any* online course-taking. Specifically, high school graduation rates were about 4 percent higher and college enrollment rates (two-year and four-year) were about 13 percent higher on average for those not taking courses online. These gaps generally increased with more years of online course-taking, where students taking courses online for four or more years had graduation rates that were roughly 14 percentage points *lower* than those with no online course-taking, and their college enrollment rates were one-fourth of those with no online course-taking. In addition, all indicators suggested that students taking online courses and continuing on to postsecondary institutions were attending lower-quality institutions. For example, students who enrolled in online courses were about 30 percentage points more likely to attend open-admissions colleges and 33 percentage points less likely to attend institutions that confer graduate degrees. Additionally, first-year retention rates and college completion rates were significantly lower (9 and 13 percentage points, respectively) as well.

That said, we found a very different pattern in associations between online course-taking and graduation rates when we used statistical modeling to account for student and school characteristics and limited our sample to only those who had failed a course in high school. In MPS, this subgroup had, on average, high school graduation rates that were about 8–12 percentage points *higher* than similar students who did not take courses online, and their two- and four-year college enrollment rates were also about 2 percentage points higher.[9] For high school administrators under pressure to achieve higher graduation rates, especially for students who are failing courses and falling behind in their progress toward graduation, a relatively inexpensive ed-tech solution like online course-taking for credit recovery could be a boon to their efforts to increase performance. However, our research also raises concerns along the lines of those conveyed by the International Association for K–12 Online Learning— that educational programming delivered online with "very low levels (if any) of teacher involvement" and that "allows schools to say students have 'passed' whether they have learned anything or not" could worsen, rather than improve, these students' outcomes in the longer-term.[10]

Supplemental, Out-of-School Digital Learning and Student Outcomes

Low-resource school districts like MPS and DISD have long relied on the federal Title I program, which provides supplemental funding to school districts with the highest concentrations of student poverty to provide extra academic assistance to their students through programs such as out-of-school tutoring. NCLB made out-of-school tutoring mandatory for schools that repeatedly failed to make adequate yearly progress toward federal proficiency targets, and as more and more school districts came under those requirements over time, digital tutoring providers rapidly increased their penetration of the K–12 public schools tutoring market. In our prior research on out-of-school tutoring under NCLB, we observed online tutoring companies serving nearly 90 percent of the participating students in DISD, and in another large urban school district, we identified a single digital provider delivering tutoring to more than ten thousand students at one time. With anywhere from two-thirds to 100 percent of the participating students free-lunch eligible, 90 percent and more students of color, and more than a third ELLs, digital tutoring was being targeted to some of the student groups most critical to ameliorating achievement gaps. Yet the wide range of approaches and formats that emerged in online tutoring settings were especially difficult for school districts to monitor, and this made it hard to ascertain which forms of digital tutoring were more or less effective in increasing student achievement and reducing achievement gaps.

Following federal waivers from NCLB, MPS drew on existing research to specify evidence-based features of its out-of-school, digital tutoring program and contract with a provider to deliver these services. In this effort, MPS prioritized elementary students who were performing below grade level. The students receiving these services were also more likely to be Black (86 percent) versus nonparticipating students (53 percent) and economically disadvantaged (93 percent eligible for free or reduced-price lunch). The digital tutoring program had a goal of delivering at least forty hours of tutoring to each student in a school year, with no more than two to three hour of tutoring per week. The district also specified an expected tutor-student ratio of one-to-two—or one-to-one, when requested by parents. Instruction was delivered entirely through an online platform outside the regular school day, and students could schedule their tutoring sessions at their convenience.[11]

As discussed in chapter 3, the online, out-of-school tutoring program had an advantage over the other forms of digital instruction that we studied in that the administrative and student management tasks involved were minimal compared with technology integration efforts in the classroom. The one-to-one or one-to-two tutor-student ratio also potentially enabled more opportunities for personalizing instruction and an emphasis on content better targeted to student needs, as well as more time for building rapport with individual students. For example, in one online tutoring session we observed, the instructor endeavored to make the content and pedagogical approach relevant and responsive to student's own life by using a book the student was reading in reference to a lesson on character development and drawing out concrete examples for discussion based on the student's own interest in the topic.

Overall, however, our observations of the online, out-of-school tutoring sessions identified only a minority of sessions with authentically student-centered or personalized instruction. When online tutors made modifications and accommodations to the lessons, they were more likely to be limited to adjusting the readability of text or the pacing of the lesson, although they sometimes also incorporated incentives to engage the students, such as playing a game at the end of a session. In addition, despite the considerably lower student-to-teacher ratio and corresponding reduced burdens of troubleshooting technology problems with devices, technical difficulties remained an acute limiting factor in the quality of learning opportunities, as this excerpt from an observation shows:

> In the first nine minutes, students were logged on and trying to get in touch with the tutor, who had not joined the session yet. The students had almost thirty-eight minutes of technical difficulties with audio, visual, or both. One parent tried to intervene twice in locating the tutor and helping her child get connected. The tutor was the primary support for learning and technical issues, but she had her own technical issues and didn't provide much support.

Despite these drawbacks, the large majority of students taking these online sessions received the intended forty hours of tutoring or close to that number, although as the excerpt above suggests, forty hours logged in may not always imply forty hours engaged in instruction. Still, with access to an adequate number of tutoring hours, students gained, on average, in both their reading and math performance on standardized achievement tests (compared to matched samples of nonparticipating students). Some of the limitations we observed in the online tutoring sessions—including instructor difficulties in troubleshooting technology and limited capabilities for individualizing and adapting the content and their instructional approach to student needs—suggested that more training and support to bolster the pedagogical and technical skills of tutors could leverage larger gains in learning for students.

Concluding Insights and Lessons

As we have shown, digital learning has the potential to improve student learning. Across the digital tools, grades, and settings, we identified a number of common factors that appeared to play a role in whether or not students gained through digital learning. First, students were more likely to make learning gains when technology was used to enhance instruction. In some classrooms, enhancing instruction meant using a tool or blended approach that increased interactivity or reimagined learning processes. In MPS, for example, some of the online courses that facilitated the highest rates of authentic learning provided students with opportunities to conduct research and apply content to their daily lives. One assignment that epitomized this type of instruction was an in-depth, math-driven assignment to create a financial budget for students' lives ten years in the future. And in a history class, a meaningful context was established through the integration of in-depth case studies and archival documents that provided an explicit link between the historical context studied and modern life. It also sometimes meant using a digital tool that increased students' engagement, such as the clickers used in DISD to allow students to respond to questions individually, which also enabled teachers to view the distribution of responses and assess whether there was general understanding or a need to re-teach content before proceeding with the lesson. Instruction was also enhanced in using digital tools to differentiate instruction, either within a given tool, or by providing students an alternative, high-quality learning task that they could complete while the teacher worked with students individually or in small groups.

Students also need sufficient time engaging with the devices or programs to realize gains in their learning. For younger students learning with tablets in the classroom, it was important for them to have a minimum of forty to sixty minutes of use in a given week to see any gains; and for students participating in online tutoring outside of school, the threshold of forty hours across the school year was key to benefiting from these services. In online course-taking at the high school level, where student self-regulation in the classroom is even more important to their progress in learning, we saw that more time actively working in a given course session (and less idle time) were directly related to successful course completion, credit accumulation, and in turn, graduation from high school.

However, delays or interruptions in technology use associated with technical difficulties or environmental constraints (e.g., poor internet connectivity, lack of technical support) were very costly in terms of time for learning, student engagement with the lessons, and the extent to which they improved their academic performance. We documented substantial losses of instructional time that not only erased any gains from technology use, but also contributed to losses in student learning compared to similar peers who were not using technology in the classroom. In addition, technical difficulties experienced in accessing or using the digital tools and programs—whether associated with teacher preparation and training or environmental constraints outside of their control, as shown in figure 5. 1—undercut teacher confidence or beliefs that the technology would enhance students' learning and thereby reduced the time allocated for technology use. At the high school level, students who experienced challenges in logging in and who lacked instructor support or attention for engaging in online learning were less likely to advance in their classes, and over time, were more likely to have their courses disabled than to complete them.

As discussed in each chapter in this book, our research has continually pointed to the importance of early and ongoing professional development that boosts teacher technology knowledge and their confidence in the properties and potential for its use to improve student learning. Teachers with this knowledge base can not only impart this information to their students and activate their engagement in learning with technology in the classroom, but they can also share it with their peers in other classrooms to bolster school-based supports and the sharing of best practices for digital learning. Greater live instructor engagement and use of blended learning approaches were also consistently found to be key to student gains through learning with technology, but our classroom observations and interviews with teachers showed that the use of these teaching strategies was closely linked to instructor technical and pedagogical capacities that need to be deliberately and actively cultivated in the rollout of digital learning initiatives. In addition, we frequently saw that students benefit when teachers have access to program resources that facilitate appropriate modifications of the technology and both the teacher and student have the capacity to make use of them. Ensuring that teachers have sufficient time and information to feel confident in implementing individualizing features also facilitates greater differentiation in technology use in the classroom that may be particularly beneficial to subgroups of students with different learning needs.

Lastly, school districts can benefit greatly from building capacities to use the data they have at hand to monitor and evaluate student use of and outcomes with technology. Some programs and tools allow teachers to monitor student engagement and progress with digital learning in real time, but teachers need to understand how to access and use the data to identify individual student needs and facilitate corresponding accommodations for more effective use. District- and school-level capacities may also need to be strengthened for monitoring student outcomes associated with technology use over time. For example, MPS was able to determine that many ninth- and tenth-graders were less prepared academically and in their motivation and self-regulation to benefit from online course-taking in high school, and the schools accordingly began to disable or discourage their participation in this program. The walk-through tools that we created for districts to monitor classroom use of educational technology can also generate information valuable for program evaluation and revamping. Using the walk-through observation instrument (see appendix B) in DISD, we were able to confirm that shifting to a "feeder pattern" model of tablet distribution and using teacher fellows to facilitate sharing of effective technology integration practices across classroom and schools appeared to contribute to not only sustained use of the tablets, but also more effective use of the tablets for student learning over time.

In the next and final chapter, we offer concrete strategies and suggestions for how school district staff, instructors, and others can act on the evidence and insights presented in this and other chapters to realize the promise of better and more equitable outcomes for the students they serve through digital learning.

CHAPTER

6

Acting on the Evidence

A S WE HAVE DESCRIBED throughout this book, many of the factors essential to (or "leverage points" for) ensuring the success of digital learning initiatives have less to do with the capabilities of the technology itself and more to do with how it is delivered in the classroom and other educational settings. In fact, the key factors to success in digital learning largely mirror predictors of effective schools more generally—knowledgeable, well-prepared teachers, innovative and collaborative instructional practices, strong, school-based administrative support, and so on. We use this concluding chapter to highlight four broad categories of important leverage points for increasing student learning:

- Policies, contracts, and budgets
- Capacity of organizations to support evaluation
- Capacity of educators to support implementation
- Student-centered and responsive pedagogy

Through discussion of these key leverage points, we reiterate the central theme of this book—that digital learning initiatives can be effective, but it takes planning, monitoring and assessment, and revamping and refinement over time to understand and cultivate preconditions under which ed-tech is effective at district, school, classroom, and student levels. Furthermore, if the learning of *all* students is going to be supported and advanced through these initiatives, then implementers at all levels of these initiatives—from planning and purchase by state and local educational leaders down to the classroom and student level where digital tools are integrated—need to attend to the equity implications and assess equity in outcomes for every decision made or practice instituted.

The description of lessons and promising practices presented in this chapter reflect on infrastructures we jointly created to build capacity at the district, school, and classroom levels to facilitate more productive evaluation of digital learning and retooling of approaches for its integration in varying educational settings. We point to resources for district and school leaders/staff and instructors who are looking for support in their technology integration efforts and want to ensure that access to and use of digital learning are equitable. We also identify actors at state, district, school, and classroom levels who can best act on the policy and program levers identified in this work to facilitate ongoing improvements in educational technology integration. Throughout the discussion of lessons below, we have highlighted key resources, strategies, and questions to guide educators and leaders in "acting on the evidence" to foster equity. Integrating digital learning is complex and challenging work, and there is no one playbook that will work for all educational entities, but it is our intent that the resources and insights shared will assist others in developing a digital learning strategy that best serves the students in each unique school context.

Most schools (90 percent of those in a RAND Education study) lack the time, resources, training, and other capacities critical for implementing high-quality digital instruction and personalizing learning.[1] In school districts with sizable numbers of low-income, high-need students, these capacity deficits are even more pressing in the day-to-day work of technology integration. Accordingly, we give particular attention to innovative tools and approaches to implementing digital learning that were developed and tried in low-resource settings, and may therefore be more readily adapted in contexts similar to those we studied. This reflects the urgency of increasing equity in digital learning and eradicating practices that exacerbate inequalities to better deliver on the promise of improving learning with technology *for all students.*

Policies, Contracts, and Budgets

Policy actions and contexts arbitrate how educational initiatives such as digital tool integration play out in schools and classrooms. For example, programs like the Federal Communications Commission E-Rate program have made possible considerable strides toward reducing the costs of telecommunications infrastructure and internet access that support access to digital learning opportunities in public schools. Yet arranging *physical* access to educational technology may be one of the least challenging components of implementing a digital learning initiative today. We have seen how crucial it is for districts to leverage the state and federal policies that support effective implementation, especially in the leverage points we discuss below (organizational capacity, educator capacity, and high-quality pedagogic approaches). For example, the Student Support and Academic Enrichment (SSAE) program, recently authorized under ESSA, recognizes this and makes funding available to state educational agencies, school districts, and schools for increasing *effective use* of technology to improve digital literacy and academic growth and achievement among students. Public schools are encouraged to use these and other federal grant funds for improving professional development, facilitating educator collaboration and communications, and increasing other supports for educators to deliver high-quality instruction.[2]

Further, if a district or school with access to Title I funding is integrating educational technology schoolwide, it can use Title I, Part A funds to purchase devices as well as other digital learning resources that can be used to support students and staff in its implementation, including assisting teachers in improving their use of effective blended learning instructional practices. In addition, Title III, Part A funds are available specifically to provide access to supplemental resources for ELLs. Given the inadequacies we have observed in the capacities of some commonly used digital tools to accommodate the needs of ELLs, we strongly encourage districts to leverage the use of these funds. Title IV, Part A funds may also be used to facilitate use of other open educational resources; and separately, rural school districts can apply for supplemental funds through the Small, Rural School Achievement Program (SRSA) and the Rural and Low-Income School Program (RLIS) to support technology integration and instructional practice in schools. We also urge school districts to reach out to university and other nonprofit organizations to probe their interest in collaborating in the implementation and evaluation of digital learning initiatives, as well as to expand the range of options for applying for foundation and other philanthropic support of these efforts.

State and local educational agencies likely have the greatest opportunity to bring more resources to their schools for educational technology integration early in the planning stages of digital learning initiatives. These resources may include financial supports, commitments for regular instructor trainings, other personnel support, supplemental programming, evaluation assistance, and more. We encourage school districts to explore opportunities for creating infrastructure with partnering organizations including prospective technology vendors, community-based organizations, and educational nonprofits (including universities) to prepare for and support the rollout, integration, and evaluation of digital learning initiatives—*in advance of any technology purchase.* For

Acting on the Evidence: Grants and Funding

We encourage state and local educational agencies to work together in exploring opportunities for leveraging these funding streams in key federal legislation for digital learning rollout and implementation:

- Federal Communications Commission E-Rate program
- Every Student Succeeds Act (ESSA): Title I, Title III, and Title IV
- Student Support and Academic Enrichment (SSAE) program
- Small, Rural School Achievement Program (SRSA)
- Rural and Low-Income School Program (RLIS)

example, school districts may be able to build many of these supports into the contract with their chosen vendor. By articulating their anticipated needs and expectations for supports during explorations and negotiations with contractors, they may be able to secure a better deal that more fully supports the work of implementing digital learning, especially in ways that are relevant and responsive to the unique communities and cultural contexts in which school districts operate.

Through these initial discussions or explorations, school districts should clarify the vendor's assumptions about district capacities for supporting the implementation of digital learning and make clear their expectations for what types of supports the vendor will provide, not only at the time of initial rollout, but also over time as technology integration proceeds. For example, instructors will need vendor support to learn how to make full use of the digital tools in the classroom, but training sessions or workshops at the start of the school year will be insufficient to support instructors (and students) as they begin to try out ways of integrating technology and gradually build knowledge for adapting instructional strategies to learning with technology. Thus, school districts could request at the time of purchase that the contact include a vendor commitment to a specific number of training hours or sessions with district staff that would continue throughout the school/contract year. School districts might also be wise to establish one-year versus multiyear contracts, or build in provisions for renegotiation of contract terms, to ensure that the level of support or commitments from the vendor can be adjusted to meet basic instructor and student needs in technology integration. Similarly, districts can embed an explicit focus on diversity and equity into contracts by clarifying a process for content review and revision both up front and when problematic content in courses is identified.

In addition, given the key role that instructors play in integrating technology at the level where students engage, involving or gathering input from teachers prior to choosing products and arranging a contract for the technology purchase could help to avoid problems of digital tools that are ill-suited to student (and instructional) needs and capacities. In

Acting on the Evidence: Contracting with Vendors

In contracting with vendors for digital tools and their implementation, state and local educational agencies should communicate expectations for the following contract provisions or terms:

- Commitment and resources to provide equal access and adaptations for all students, including ELLs and students with special educational needs.
- Provision of ongoing training for educators related to:
  - Implementing digital tools in the most effective way for their particular context
  - Ensuring that the digital tool promotes equity in access and outcomes across groups of students
  - Addressing technical problems that commonly arise
  - Promoting equitable instructional practices, such as encouraging student help-seeking and supplementing digital content with authentic work in blended instruction
- Agreement to share data collected within the tool for the district's own analysis and use in process improvement, including disaggregation by student group.
- Demonstration of the ways in which the technology ensures cultural awareness, relevance, and responsiveness in the instructional materials.
- Commitment from the vendor and/or digital tool developer to receive and act on feedback on cultural awareness, relevance, and responsiveness in the instructional materials, including youth and family voices in the decision-making and review processes

our work with school districts, we have found that instructional staff, through their daily interactions with students and their own explorations of alternative strategies for engaging students in ed-tech use, acquire a keen sense of what is beneficial or constraining for their effective use of digital tools. For example, teachers are often able to identify the limitations of technology in adapting to student reading levels or English-learning skills. Teachers could be given the opportunity to try out technology in educational settings before a purchase is made, and school districts could also create teacher feedback loops or channels for communicating early feedback on how digital tools are working for their students and for the achievement of learning objectives. And for districts in which technology purchases and use have been more decentralized, district staff might also first consider allocating resources to conduct an inventory of technology in use or a districtwide needs assessment to inform the next educational technology purchase.

It is also imperative that district leaders, vendors, and educators work together at the outset of digital learning initiatives to explicitly develop guidelines and designate resources for promoting and supporting equity in access, use, and outcomes of technology integration. Applying an equity lens to the use of technology in the classroom also means looking closely at which students (disaggregated by important social identities like race and class) tend to be involved in certain digital initiatives, and whether this is purposeful and/or perpetuates opportunity gaps. For example, we saw the potential pitfalls of grouping students by their ability—for instance, by their academic performance or facility with technology—in supporting positive interactions between instructors, students, and the devices. The types of spaces that are allocated for learning with technology and the ease or level of interaction between instructors and students that they facilitate are also factors that may affect equity in opportunities for learning, particularly for students who are less comfortable with or inclined to request help from their instructor.[3]

District staff and educators should also explore opening discussions about anti-racist, social justice principles for guiding the implementation of digital learning initiatives, including providing teachers with skills and strategies for initiating conversations with their students about racial and socioeconomic inequities present in their educational and community settings.[4] And students should be empowered to recognize and report their concerns about inequitable or discriminatory treatment that they experience (or see others subjected to) in their learning environments. We observed a range of content in digital learning environments—some better than others, of course. Yet when students, especially those from historically marginalized groups, experience racial stereotypes in online course content, it not only affects their opportunities to learn, but it can also be harmful to their emotional well-being. Creating a space for students to provide input on content is one way to engage students in anti-racist, social justice efforts and to voice their perceptions of and objections to curricular content that lacks real-world relevance or authentic work.

In sum, state and local educational agencies need to be prepared to invest more in the non-technology "inputs" or infrastructure essential to the successful and equitable integration of technology in schools, which will require higher-level and systemwide efforts and coordination to better meet the educational needs of *all* students engaged in digital learning.

Capacity of Organizations to Evaluate Technology Integration

School districts today feel constant financial pressure from increasingly tight budgets, mounting pension costs, and federal mandates for spending that are imposed without funding to match them. More than one-half of school principals and district-level administrators who participated in a nationally representative survey reported that higher levels of student need were also a major factor contributing to their growing per-pupil expenditures.[5] In the face of rising educational costs and pressing student needs that limit the resources available for evaluation of educational initiatives, opportunities to form collaborations with universities, community-based partners, and other nonprofit organizations can support districts in monitoring and evaluation efforts. In the context of digital learning initiatives, we recommend that school districts invite vendors into these collaborations as well.

For example, to facilitate more informative internal and independent evaluations of the implementation of digital learning initiatives, we suggest that prior to signing any contracts for the purchase or support of educational technology integration, school districts (or schools) should establish data-sharing agreements with vendors and/or evaluation partners that specify access to information that the vendor may collect on student technology use, as well as the processes for actually sharing the data (e.g., point people from each organization, time lines, data transfer protocols). These data, especially when linked to student information in school records, can provide richer insights and understanding of which students are using the technology (and how), and important patterns related to student identifications such as race, language status, and others. School districts should request a description of the data that the vendor regularly collects about student use of its technology and specify in a contract for technology purchases the data fields they would like to receive and in what form. The contracting (and/or collaborating) parties should also specify in advance how the vendor data will be linked to student school records (such as a procedure for securely linking student identifiers (IDs) with technology user IDs), whether the district or the vendor will create that link, and how the data will be securely stored and accessed for analysis. University or other education nonprofit partners may be a valuable source of support in making these contractual and data-access arrangements and in performing subsequent data preparation, programming, and analysis work.

In addition, school districts may benefit from opening their school doors to independent evaluation efforts by granting evaluation staff and partners access to classrooms and other educational settings where digital tools are being integrated into instruction. We developed four instruments for understanding technology use in the classroom or other settings (including online observations) that are freely available through our study website. The first is an observation instrument for whole-class or individual student observations (see appendix A) that is intended for longer, more in-depth observations (e.g., lasting for half or all of a class or instructional period). The second is a walk-through tool that is intended to capture a "point in time" picture of whether and how educational technology is being accessed and used in an educational setting (see appendix B). The third and fourth tools are for evaluating the cultural relevance and responsiveness of online courses (appendix C) and the extent to which curricular content and instructional activities in online course videos and assignments facilitate authentic work (appendix D). Any of

Acting on the Evidence: Facilitating an Evaluation Infrastructure

Reflecting that technology integration requires continuous monitoring, evaluating, and revamping to fine-tune and improve implementation and outcomes, we recommend facilitating an evaluation infrastructure to guide these efforts as follows:

- As a key part of an equity-focused school system, districts and vendors should adopt an organizational culture and structural approach focused on opening their "doors and databases" for evaluation and learning.
- With research and evaluation partners, create purposeful structures, such as those illustrated in this book, to support constant feedback loops for learning and acting on information generated through monitoring and evaluation efforts.
- To ensure representation of diverse voices and perspectives, engage a range of stakeholders (e.g., teachers, students, family, community-based partners) in evaluating needs, choosing digital tools, and understanding barriers to and facilitators of implementation.

these tools can be used by district or school staff to gain insights into the quality of the digital tools for learning and both challenges instructors are encountering and best practices in technology integration that can then be shared with other instructors. In fact, some of the promising practices that we observed were developed in response to problems around or impediments to student learning with technology that instructors had identified and sought to overcome.

Capacity of Educators to Support Implementation

It is nothing new in educational research to claim that teachers matter greatly to student success. Yet understanding the *ways* in which teachers matter gets more complex when looking at digital learning. As we showed in chapter 3, the proximity and role of teachers can shift in relation to decisions about curricular content, the actual instruction,

Acting on the Evidence: Tools for Evaluating the Integration of Digital Tools

We are publicly and freely sharing the tools we developed and applied in our research-practice partnerships for evaluating the integration of digital tools in classrooms and other educational settings. These can be found in appendixes A, B, C, and D; a downloadable copy is available on our study website (https://my.vanderbilt.edu/digitaled/methods/):

- *Classroom Observation Instrument* (appendix A): This tool requires more time for observation in the educational setting, largely because it examines in greater detail the roles and approaches of the instructor and students in using digital tools, as well as various aspects of the classroom or instructional environment that may support or impede learning with the technology. For example, it is through this tool that we began to understand potential patterns in which groups of students tended to seek assistance from in-person instructors to help them progress through online course content. The observer rates interactions between the instructor, the student, and the digital tool, including the form and nature of their interactions (e.g., instructional model, assessment activities), the level of engagement of the instructor and students, the curricular content and structure, and features of the physical environment that might increase or limit student access to and effective use of digital tools.
- *Classroom Walk-Through Instrument* (appendix B): This tool is for a quicker, in-person overview of the types of digital tools in use and how they are being used in the educational setting, including information on their functionality and instructional strategies and practices observed at the time of the walk-through. This type of examination is designed to be for a wider, surface scrape of practices and implementation to help districts and schools map overall patterns in the integration of digital tools. We suggest using this instrument to focus on patterns in *which types* of students are engaging with *what tools* and *how*. For example, one might explore if only certain subgroups of students have access to more authentic, engaging, project-based blended learning initiatives, while others tend to be in front of asynchronous, remedial "drill-and-kill" tools.

- *Cultural Relevance and Responsiveness Instrument* (appendix C): Like the Classroom Observation Instrument (appendix A), this tool requires considerable time if districts are interested in doing a full analysis. Our purpose in using it was to assess the level of cultural relevance and responsiveness in online or digital courses. With many digital learning tools, online content is primarily viewed or experienced only by students. Our team went through entire online courses and rated each module with a separate form, based on a rubric, and then wrote in-depth descriptive notes using prompts, which allowed for greater opportunity to shine light on potentially biased or discriminatory content in online courses. Educators could also use the tool to do shorter digital "walk-throughs" of course content, for example, to scan for promising or problematic content.
- *Authentic Online Work Rubric* (appendix D): This rubric enables users to evaluate the extent to which online courses provide opportunities for higher-order thinking and real-world relevance, two primary components of authentic work identified in prior research. The higher-order thinking scale component of the rubric is designed to measure the extent to which students are asked to think deeply and critically about course content and to generate new knowledge. The real-world relevance scale aims to identify the extent to which course content resonates with or is applicable to students' lives, interests, and/or aspirations. This tool could be used formatively to determine if a given technology vendor's course offerings are suitable to a particular student population, as well as for ongoing evaluation of the quality of online learning opportunities provided to students.

and even to the needs of students themselves. In fact, the most effective use of digital learning often requires more and different, not less, investment and adaptation from teachers. Effective digital integration of digital tools requires districts and schools to consider and plan for how expectations of teachers' roles and responsibilities will change when introducing technology into the classroom. Those involved in introducing and implementing digital instructional tools should not only be skilled in using them, but also have ongoing and consistent support to make sure it is working for *all* students. Teachers' (and students') understandings of how the technology functions is key in determining how they will use the tools—in both intended and unintended ways. Building the capacity of adults (instructors as well as parents) to effectively use digital tools requires ongoing access to professional training for the planning and use of the technology, as well as time for practicing with the tools and communicating with others about effective strategies for their use. Our research illustrates how this plays out through three important channels: who is put into instructional roles, their professional development, and their sense of efficacy (i.e., do they believe they can make a change through digital learning?). In our years of studying digital learning in multiple district sites, we observed a breadth of contexts in which digital tools are used and identified patterns in the types of roles classroom teachers are expected to undertake when integrating technology. These included providing tech support to both students and other teachers, administrative responsibilities to enroll and log students into the digital platforms, behavioral management while students use digital tools, content support, and employing digital platforms to assess student learning. The diversity of roles played and skills demanded by these programs suggests it matters greatly who is placed into support positions—what teaching certifications they have, technology certifications, content expertise, experience with student populations, and more. Yet staffing practices sometimes showed a sharp contrast to the reality of these demands and expectations, with new or substitute teachers consigned to classrooms or technology labs with inadequate training and support for these roles, and some students largely left on their own to navigate learning with technology. We need to give further consideration to how students in low-resource settings tend to disproportionately experience conditions such as new and/or substitute teachers who have not received the necessary supports for implementing digital learning.

In terms of the training and outlook of educators for digital learning, it should be a precondition of any digital learning initiative that teachers have the knowledge and skills to provide basic technical support

Acting on the Evidence: Supporting Teachers in Implementing Digital Learning

Instructional expenditures are the largest component of school district budgets and subject to efficiency considerations in planning, but the objective of economizing should not dominate decisions for personnel and staffing. We suggest:

- Hiring decisions should consider the full scope of work in integrating digital tools and evaluate staff for the expertise and experience required in making digital learning initiatives successful.
- School districts should consider the types of alternative certifications that might be a better fit for instructors who will be engaging students in digital learning across multiple content areas.
- Districts should examine opportunities for economies of scale that could be realized across schools or districts; for example, creating a "call center" staffed by educators who know both the digital tools platform and the educational content to provide more timely support relevant to specific content areas or student populations (e.g., ELLs, students with disabilities).

to students, such as maintaining internet connectivity and addressing hardware and software challenges. In fact, we found that teachers' baseline technology expertise (and subsequent growth in expertise from the beginning to the end of the school year) were positively associated with student engagement and achievement gains through technology use. We also learned that the technical features of digital tools can play a substantial role in shaping student experiences. Teachers leading the more successful classroom technology integration understand how to best leverage the strengths of the tools and supplement the limitations of these features. In fact, we also found that blended learning strategies yield the most engaging and promising opportunities to learn; indeed, many digital tools are predicated on the assumption they will be used in a blended approach. That said, in the majority of settings in low-resource contexts, teachers need greater and more tailored capacity-building around how to set up and implement blended learning environments and instructional practices.

Moreover, research suggests the importance of providing training and guidance for teachers that is not focused solely on the technology itself, but rather demonstrates how to use technology within teachers' specific content areas and/or grade levels, so that they can more readily transfer that knowledge through innovative uses of technology.[6] We found that teachers' beliefs in the efficacy of technology for student learning increased their use of blended instruction and the overall intensity of technology use in the classroom, which in turn provides a higher-quality experience for students. In addition, many teachers will need support and training for working with students who themselves may have limited experience with using digital tools or require accommodations in learning that may not be fully met by a given digital tool; for example, in interviews, teachers frequently pointed out the limitations of the digital tools for English translation or for adapting content to the range of reading levels in a given educational setting. Furthermore, for students who may not have a level of self-regulation that is anticipated by software designers for technology use, teachers may need support in tailoring and allocating individual student supports in the classroom in ways that ensure *equity* in learning opportunities (as opposed to simply responding *equally* to student requests). Lastly, we know from research in traditional classroom settings that building the capacity of teachers to develop and deliver culturally responsive teaching is also central to equitable opportunities and outcomes for all students. This absolutely applies in digital settings, where teachers need to have training specific not only to developing and working with digital tools in culturally responsive ways, but also for being able to identify and mitigate content when it is culturally inappropriate, biased, and/or discriminatory.

In sum, the right fit of personnel with position, professional development, and belief in the ability of digital instruction to increase learning gave teachers more of a "toolkit" to take advantage of the different capabilities of a particular platform and to deal with the unexpected in practice.

Acting on the Evidence: Professional Development and Training to Support Digital Learning

The critical role for professional development and training to support digital learning initiatives was a constant refrain in our analysis and findings, and we highlight some of the most promising strategies below:

- Cultivate and support peer-to-peer coaching (e.g., digital teacher fellows) as a cost-efficient, timely, and potentially scalable approach for facilitating increased support for digital learning and exchange.
- Develop student peer support, such as students identified as "tech helpers" in the classroom, to reduce tech-management challenges and promote student engagement in digital learning.
- Conduct a needs assessment with current instructors to identify specific areas where additional training is most needed (apart from digital tool platform support).
- With support from the technology vendor, ensure district technical support staff have the requisite skills to conduct professional development training sessions throughout the school years.
- Provide pedagogic training on digital tools (beyond how to access data and navigate platforms) to:
  - Increase student engagement in blended learning settings
  - Facilitate higher-order thinking via digital tools
  - Incorporate offline materials into instruction that enhance digital and blended learning opportunities
- Explore what types of training district and school administration and staff need in order to ensure digital tools are culturally responsive to the communities they serve.

Student-Centered and Responsive Pedagogy That Generates Authentic Student Work

In examining the teaching approaches in classrooms where digital tools are being integrated, we have focused on both the curricular content and instructional strategies. We have observed that equitable learning opportunities and outcomes are enhanced when pedagogy is student centered and responsive to students' needs, identities, and contexts. Student-centered learning should inform both the curriculum framework and the instructional or pedagogic strategy. A frequent criticism of the implementation of digital tools in K–12 classrooms is that they often are used to simply substitute for or supplement traditional instructional strategies and curriculum materials, such as replacing a print resource with a digitally accessed worksheet that doesn't alter or improve on how students learn.[7] In fact, research generally finds that many teacher adaptations of technology have been incremental and directed primarily at more efficiently carrying out their usual instructional and curricular strategies. However, in addition to innovative curriculum structures, instructional models applied in digital learning that are truly transformative should engage students in new ways that would not be possible without the technology and that adapt to student-specific needs and abilities.

School districts with a goal of implementing more student-centered instructional approaches should give consideration to the following insights from research and practice. First, there is an important distinction between *individualized* learning and *personalized* learning; and it is the latter that promotes the most effective student-centered approaches. Of the digital tools we observed, most facilitated some elements of individualized learning, where students each had their own device and worked on software or programs at their own pace. In some cases, the platforms allowed for the choice and progression of learning activities to be adaptable based on the students' level of proficiency (via initial and/or ongoing assessment); this becomes an important way of centering student needs. Within those platforms of individualized learning, we occasionally observed personalized learning experiences, where instruction and curriculum were responsive to students' learning needs, interests, and contexts and students had the opportunity to lead the learning process. *Accessibility* is likewise key to centering student needs; for example, whether written text or audio is available in languages other than English. Relatedly, the simple practice of regular check-ins between students and teachers—both on personal and academic issues—allowed teachers

Acting on the Evidence: Improving Personalized and Blended Learning Experiences

We encourage adoption of the following practices of *district* and *school leaders* to improve the quality and cultural responsiveness of content and increase opportunities for personalized and blended learning experiences:

- Select digital learning–based tools and programs that facilitate the options and accommodations for customization that meet the needs of your student population.
- Set clear expectations and increase resources and support for the integration of blended learning techniques that leverage the benefits of both face-to-face and technology-based learning.
- Carefully deliberate and continually reassess which students are assigned to what types of digital learning opportunities to ensure alignment between program features and students' educational needs, and reflect on unintended but important patterns in which groups of students regularly have access to more enriching learning versus those who do not.
- Work with vendors of digital tools to design better courses and applications, with an eye toward making them more responsive to the cultures, contexts, and lived experiences of the students they serve and toward increasing student engagement.
- Require external curricular reviews to involve individuals who are diverse and representative of the student populations served. Consider bringing student representatives onto review panels who also are compensated as experts in their own experiences and learning needs.

to personalize more of the instruction around students and their needs. This could mean using "floating" or rotating time when students are on devices to do informal verbal check-ins. It also could mean establishing measurable, weekly guidelines for student progress that are rewarded through seemingly small ways, like acknowledging students' positive progress on a whiteboard or with certificates of completion.

We also encourage districts and vendors to work together in making decisions about the format, models, and curricular structure that will best support teaching with digital tools, as there are trade-offs for each of these components in relation to facilitating student-centered instruction. For example, a software-based, asynchronous platform may better facilitate adjusting to students' scheduling needs for supplemental instruction (e.g., it can be used at home at any time of the day), but it is less able to adapt to students' specific and evolving learning needs.

A central element of being student centered is not only ensuring that teaching approaches are responsive to the learning needs of students, but also to their cultural identities and contexts. Research in traditional, face-to-face classrooms offers important lessons for the potential of culturally responsive curriculum to transform the educational experiences and outcomes of students, particularly those from historically marginalized groups.[8] We applied this concept to map the different types of cultural responsiveness and relevance observed within selected digital tools, examining how social messages related to the culture of power are perpetuated, acknowledged, or disrupted.[9] In doing so, we documented both limitations and opportunities for cultural responsiveness and disrupting dominant cultural narratives within digital learning platforms. For example, a language arts course on mythology not only talked about the histories and stories of the Maasai people in Africa, but also talked about their present-day communities in Kenya and Tanzania. It then followed with deeper questions for students, asking them to reflect on their own cultures and whether there are traditions embedded to help explain natural phenomena. This not only brings more diverse communities and cultures into a discussion of mythology, but resists "historicizing" them by also focusing on present-day communities, and it prompts a level of self-reflection that encourages critical thinking about the content. Given the importance of cultural responsiveness to student success, it suggests district and schools should make purposeful decisions around the most appropriate use of digital tools in the classroom, so that it doesn't replace other instructional approaches that might be able to more successfully integrate culturally responsive approaches.

Acting on the Evidence: Improving Cultural Responsiveness and Personalized and Blended Learning Experiences

We encourage adoption of the following practices of *classroom educators* to improve the quality and cultural responsiveness of content and increase opportunities for personalized and blended learning experiences:

- Review the digital content and tools and ask for demo access to see what the content looks like before adopting or implementing it in your class.
- Ask students what they think of the digital content and show them that you value their feedback on the tools you choose and use.
- Look for leverage points in the digital platform or device where teachers can inject their own content and assignments, especially in ways that enhance its relevance and responsiveness to the communities and cultural contexts of the students they serve.
- Collaborate with teachers in the district who are working with the same digital content or tools to create a shared space (e.g., a collaborative online folder) for supplementary/support materials, as well as professional development opportunities.
- Think about low-resource-intensive ways to track student progress and provide positive recognition; for example:
  - Regular data chats with students
  - Positive, concrete rewards for student success, such as informing caregivers of positive achievements and posting names of students who achieve milestones
  - Regular celebrations or awards ceremony for student achievements that include an invitation to students, families, and other teachers

Conclusion: Acting on the Evidence and Realizing the Promise

Throughout this book, we have investigated and illustrated the promise of digital learning with attention to three main axes of digital learning initiatives that can have profound implications for equity in educational opportunities and quality:

- *Who* in public elementary and secondary schools is directed to use digital learning tools and for what purpose
- *How* digital learning is implemented at school and classroom levels, including the infrastructure, environment, and supports provided to teachers and students and how it changes their role and engagement in the educational process
- *What* educational content is accessed through digital learning tools, including in blended forms

In concluding, we come back to these three central axes to highlight insights and promising practices from the evidence that can guide educators as they navigate their own efforts to integrate digital tools in the context of an equity imperative.

Who Is Directed to Use Which Tools for What Purpose

It is more common than not for school districts to roll out digital learning initiatives with the goal to remedy "gaps" in both access and achievement, with the idea that technology can personalize or tailor learning to the needs of students who are academically, economically, or historically disadvantaged in our school systems. Sometimes digital tools are also seen as a less expensive alternative to strategies such as hiring more teachers or classroom aides or intensifying other classroom- and campus-based supports to improve the quality of learning opportunities for students. Our research clearly shows, however, that the students prioritized for digital learning are likely to need more, not less, of everything that schools and teachers typically do in the classroom to support student learning when they are given the opportunity to learn online or with devices. For example, live instructor assistance and one-to-one content learning support can be even more critical for students when the primary source of instructional delivery is an asynchronous video or an application on a tablet. Students with less prior technology experience or access to devices in their homes may also need more instructor support in using features of technology that are intended to be adaptable to students' individual needs, such as features that allow them to modify the pace of instruction or get support with definitions of words or language translation. At the same time, our research also showed that the students most in need of these extra supports may be the least inclined to ask for assistance in the classroom.

Given these realities, districts and schools should plan, to the extent possible, for lower student-to-teacher ratios (rather than the higher student-to-teacher ratios we sometimes observed) in educational settings where digital learning is being introduced. For example, in a high school in Milwaukee that was designed specifically to better meet the special needs of opportunity youth (for example, those who might be pregnant or parenting), we observed comparatively low student-teacher ratios and ready access to both content and technical support from live instructors for students taking courses online. In the example from chapter 3, a teacher who had an unexpectedly large class of students due to another teacher's absence creatively used student groupings and pairings in a series of varied and blended instructional strategies to fully engage them in the lesson and to provide opportunities for them to learn together in using the devices. Some teachers also identified student technology helpers to increase the time and support available for all students in learning on the devices. Successfully supporting students in learning with technology, as well as in overcoming barriers that have impeded their progress in school, places additional role and skill demands on teachers that need to be recognized at school and district levels. If school districts are not prepared to acknowledge and provide for the substantial level of instructor time and support that is required to deliver quality learning opportunities to the students directed to digital learning, then we encourage educational leaders to take a step back and rethink their options for using digital learning to reduce gaps in access and student educational outcomes. This would be preferred to risking the "ugly" side of digital learning that we occasionally saw, such as when an instructor in an online classroom matter-of-factly and resignedly commented in the presence of his students, "There is no learning happening here."

How Digital Learning Is Implemented

The array of choices that school districts face in deciding on the type of educational technology to adopt for a specific grade level or subgroup of students can be overwhelming, but as suggested above, "getting it right" should be less the focus in these initial decisions than "committing the resources to implementing it well." The lessons from our work with two large, urban school districts suggest that planning at the outset to expect and leverage concrete contributions from education technology vendors, school district technology staff and school leaders, teachers, and other community partners toward the effective implementation and ongoing monitoring, evaluation, and refining of technology integration efforts will be critical to realizing the promise of these initiatives. In Dallas, for example, the school district benefited from a foundation partner that not only helped to underwrite the cost of purchasing·tablets for elementary schools, but also worked closely with the schools where the tablets were being integrated to continuously improve the professional development offered to teachers and the technical support available on campuses. This more intensive level of support was necessarily time-limited, however, and it was therefore incumbent on the district and school staff to support the sharing and sustainability of the best practices developed with the support of their implementing partner. These efforts to increase the capacity and self-efficacy of teachers in integrating and blending the use of tablets in their daily lessons led to higher-quality (i.e., more engaging, authentic, and responsive) instructional experiences and student learning gains with more intensive device use.

In Milwaukee, district staff worked to establish contractual agreements with technology vendors that facilitated the sharing of data collected by the vendors through students' use of the digital tools. These data were used to better understand patterns of student technology use, such as which students were making progress (or not) toward their educational goals, and to inform district- and school-level policies regarding who would be assigned to digital learning and how they could be better supported. MPS, for instance, largely discontinued the practice of assigning students in the ninth grade to repeat courses in the online credit recovery program, after becoming aware that they were often unprepared in terms of their reading level and the self-regulation required to make steady progress toward completion. District staff also used teacher professional development sessions to communicate what they were learning from the analysis of data on student technology use and from teacher-developed strategies to increase student progress, with the goal of expanding the use of effective practices for technology integration throughout the district. The "teacher fellows" program piloted in MPS to promote the sharing of innovative practices developed in the classroom is an example of another strategy that can be instituted early in the introduction of a digital tool and scaled up as implementation and learning about what works well takes place.

What Educational Content Is Being Accessed Through Digital Tools

As a central element of the instructional core, the content around which teachers and students interact to facilitate learning becomes even more powerful in digital settings where the places that house it (e.g., software, web-based programs) often drive actual instruction.[10] Our study suggests promising practices to improve the quality and responsiveness of the content accessed with digital tools. First, it is critically important for educators at the classroom, school, and district level to have a clear understanding of the nature of digital content itself. Just as walk-throughs and textbook reviews make non-digital content more visible, teachers and administrators need to develop systematic ways to get inside the "black box" of online content that typically only students see. This is equally true for educational researchers partnering with schools and districts. For example, as part of our research-practice partnership, MPS brings together people from across different district offices—including Curriculum and Instruction, Assessment, Extended Learning Opportunities, Advanced Learning, and Research and Evaluation—to discuss insights from our analyses. Furthermore, aided by our investigation of the cultural responsiveness of digital content, district staff have partnered with a vendor to strategize ways in which they can connect their own curricular review processes to better examine the digital content that vendors provide under contract, with an eye toward ensuring equity in access for all students (e.g., the presence of language options for English learner), cultural appropriateness and responsiveness (e.g., the recognition of racial stereotypes), and alignment to district content (e.g., the use of particular literacy strategies in elementary grades).

Another promising practice focuses on building teacher capacity related to content with the right mix of training, allowing them to not only match particular digital resources with particular student needs, but to also integrate their own educational content. Among other things, this allows for the content to be more relevant and responsive to students' needs and cultural contexts. For example, in partnership with the Jiv Daya Foundation, DISD provided classroom teachers with ongoing professional development over multiple years on how best to use the tablet readers to access content in ways that would facilitate quality learning opportunities. We observed teachers adjusting and adding to online programs, including developing their own bilingual and supplementary content in order to make the digital content more accessible to all students. Importantly, many of these teachers became experts in integrating digital learning–based tools into blended instructional environments to enhance (versus supplement) traditional learning experiences.

Over the course of our study, we have seen both the pitfalls of digital learning initiatives and their potential to improve learning opportunities, student engagement, and achievement. The promise of digital tools lies within particular conditions that have to be purposefully cultivated at district, school, classroom, and student levels, from the time when they are first considered for purchase and ongoing as they are integrated into educational settings. Our hope is that through a focus on identifying and explicating the levers on which districts can act to realize this promise and the axes of equity that are critical to attend to as digital learning is implemented, we will have helped educational leaders, teachers, and other staff to discover their own pathways toward achieving greater levels of educational quality, equity, and success with digital learning. We realize there is no universal or one-size-fits all approach to doing this, yet given the rapid spread and scale of digital tools in K–12 education, the imperative to find concrete ways to do better in ensuring equity of opportunity and outcomes for all students couldn't be greater. As researchers and evaluators, we, too, have to commit to supporting our educational partners in looking deeply and specifically at how digital tools perpetuate or disrupt persistent patterns in inequity and in bringing to light both the successes and failures in digital learning that can inform the pathway forward to the best possible outcomes for students.

A

Classroom Observation Instrument

Context for Instructional Session

Q1 Date of observation: _____

Time of observation: _____

Q2 School district: _____ Other: _____

Q3 Site: _____

Q4 Location of instruction:

☐ Home   ☐ Study hall
☐ School library   ☐ Community library
☐ Core classroom   ☐ Intervention classroom
☐ Computer lab   ☐ Out-of-school-time program
☐ Unknown   ☐ Other (specify) _____

Q5 Observer 1: _____ Observer 2: _____

Q6 Type of observation:

☐ Individual student   ☐ Small group
☐ Whole class   ☐ Other: _____

Q7 Notes on instructional grouping:

Participants in Instructional Session

Q8 Notes on students' gender: _____

Q9 Notes on students' race/ethnicity: _____

Q10 Students' grade level (can enter grade or elementary/middle/high:

_____

Q11 Student(s)' language status (may check more than one):
- ☐ Official bilingual classroom
- ☐ Language other than English used
- ☐ No indication of ELL status

Q12 Notes on language status: _____

Q13 Student(s)' Disability Status:
- ☐ Accommodations or modifications observed
- ☐ No accommodations or modifications observed
- ☐ Unable to determine if accommodations or modifications were made

Q14 Notes on disability status: _____

Q15 Notes on instructor gender: _____

Q16 Notes on instructor(s)' race/ethnicity: _____

Q17 Instructor(s)' professional background: _____

_____

Instructor(s)' role during session: _____

_____

Use of Time in Instructional Session

Q18 Total times

_____ Instructional time	_____ Face-to-face
_____ Total time on task	_____ Remotely
_____ Total time student interacts with a live instructor	_____ Procedures/transition
_____ Total observation time	

Q19 Notes for time off-task:

Q20 Total time spent in instructional formats:
_____ All face-to-face   _____ Asynchronous
_____ All digital   _____ Software driven
_____ Blended   _____ Live instructor driven
_____ Synchronous

Q21 Time spent on curricular content:
_____ Math   _____ Social Studies
_____ Reading   _____ Science
_____ Writing   _____ Technology
_____ Other: _____

Q22 Time spent related to particular instructional expectations:
_____ Skill introduction   _____ Assessment
_____ Drilling/practice   _____ Games
_____ Review of previously taught lesson
_____ Enrichment/accelerated instruction
_____ Other (specify): _____

Q23 Notes on instructional expectations: _____

_____

Functionality of and Access to Technology

Q24 Technology in use by instructor (Select all that apply)

☐ Desktop   ☐ Laptop   ☐ Tablet   ☐ Smart board
☐ Projector   ☐ Document camera   ☐ None   ☐ Other _____

Q25 Was the instructor's technology functional?

☐ Yes   ☐ No   ☐ Not Applicable

Q26 Notes on functionality of instructor's technology: _____

_____

Q27 Technology in use by student(s)

☐ Desktop   ☐ Laptop   ☐ Tablet
☐ None   ☐ Other _____

Q28 Was the students' technology functional?

☐ Yes   ☐ No   ☐ Not Applicable

Q29 Notes on functionality of students' technology: _____

_____

Q30 Technology:

Total time lost to technical problems (number of minutes) _____

Number of students on each digital instruction device (number only)

____

Digital Tool in Practice

Q31 Physical environment

[How and where students access the instructional setting, including the technological setting and any associated limitations, and who else in the same physical environment as the student could assist with technological problems and support learning]

☐ [4] Students have full access to the instructional setting throughout the session.

☐ [3] The physical environment presents occasional or partial enhancements to quality learning opportunities.

☐ [2] The physical environment does not get in the way of quality learning opportunities, but does not contribute to them.

☐ [1] The physical environment presents occasional or partial barriers to quality learning opportunities.

☐ [0] The physical environment is a significant barrier to quality learning opportunities.

☐ Not applicable.

☐ Not enough information.

Q32 Comments:

Q33 Technology and digital tools

[How students access instruction, including internet connectivity; hardware and software in use; and the safety, operability, and accessibility of the technology]

☐ [4] Students have full access to the instructional setting throughout the session.

☐ [3] Students have access to the instructional setting throughout most of the session.

☐ [2] Students have access to the instructional setting throughout some the session.

☐ [1] Students had multiple problems accessing the instructional setting throughout the session.

☐ [0] No students were able to access the instructional setting.

☐ Not applicable.

☐ Not enough information.

Q34 Comments:

Q35 Curricular content and structure

[Content and skill focus, who developed it, and where it is located; learning objectives, sequence, and structure; level of rigor/intellectual challenge; ability to meet/adapt curricular content to student needs]

☐ [4] Curricular content and structure observed to create quality learning opportunities throughout the session.

☐ [3] Curricular content or structure observed to create quality learning opportunities throughout the session.

☐ [2] Curricular content or structure observed to create quality learning opportunities occasionally during the session.

☐ [1] Neither curricular content nor structure observed to create or inhibit quality learning opportunities.

☐ [0] Curricular content or structure inhibit quality learning opportunities throughout the session.

☐ Not applicable.

☐ Not enough information.

Q36 Comments:

Q37 Instructional model and tasks

[Role of instructor and software in instruction; purpose or target of instruction; student/instructor ratio and grouping patterns, multimodal instruction; order of thinking required and application of technology in instructional tasks; and ability to meet/adapt instructional model and tasks to student needs]

☐ [4] The instructional model and tasks consistently facilitate quality learning opportunities and adapt to observed (or known) student needs.

☐ [3] The instructional model and tasks mostly facilitate quality learning opportunities and adapt to observed (or known) student needs.

☐ [2] The instructional model and tasks facilitate some quality learning opportunities but do not adapt to observed (or known) student needs.

☐ [1] The instructional model and tasks do not facilitate quality learning opportunities and do not adapt to observed (or known) student needs.

☐ [0] The instructional model and tasks inhibit quality learning opportunities and do not adapt to observed (or known) student needs.

☐ Not applicable.

☐ Not enough information.

Q38 Comments:

Q39 Interaction

[How much interaction with a live person? Does the technology affect the ability of the instructor or student to positively interact with one another and the instructional resources? Constructive (contributes to learning) or destructive (deters from learning) interaction]

☐ [4] Instructors and resources have constant, constructive interaction with students.

☐ [3] Instructors and resources mostly have constant, constructive interaction with students.

☐ [2] Instructors or resources have some constructive interaction with students.

☐ [1] Instructors and resources have no constructive interaction with students.

☐ [0] Students, instructors, or resources have destructive interaction with one another.

☐ Not applicable.

☐ Not enough information.

Q40 Comments:

Q54 Digital citizenship

[Is technology being used as intended by the instructor and/or instructional program?]

☐ [4] All students are using the technology as intended by the instructor and/or instructional program.

☐ [3] Most students are acting responsibly and using the technology in intended ways, and there are no apparent distractions.

☐ [2] Some students are using the technology in unintended ways but distractions are minimal.

☐ [1] A sizable fraction of students are using the technology in unintended ways and creating distractions in the environment.

☐ [0] Most students are violating intended uses of the technology (e.g., switching to games, using for inappropriate material) and creating distractions in the environment.

☐ Not applicable.

☐ Not enough information.

Q55 Comments:

Q41 Student engagement

[Overall student engagement levels (passive or active), level of student self-regulation and persistence, and level of community within the instructional setting]

☐ [4] Students have full engagement in instruction.
☐ [3] Students are engaged in most of the instruction.
☐ [2] Students are engaged in some of the instruction.
☐ [1] Students rarely are engaged in instruction.
☐ [0] Students are not engaged in instruction.
☐ Not applicable.
☐ Not enough information.

Q42 Comments:

Q43 Instructor engagement

[Overall instructor engagement levels (passive or active) and instructor efforts to encourage engagement]

☐ [4] All instructors have full engagement in instruction.
☐ [3] Instructors are engaged in most of the instruction.
☐ [2] Instructors are engaged in some of the instruction.
☐ [1] Instructors rarely are engaged in instruction.
☐ [0] Instructors are not engaged in instruction.
☐ Not applicable.
☐ Not enough information.

Q44 Comments:

Q45 Alignment

[Alignment of instruction and curriculum to state or district standards or to other instructional settings or to stated learning objectives (including within the session and between in-person and digital instruction)]

☐ [4] All learning opportunities are fully aligned.
☐ [3] Most learning opportunities are fully aligned.

☐ [2] Most learning opportunities are partly aligned.

☐ [1] Learning opportunities are aligned for portions of the session.

☐ [0] Learning opportunities lack alignment.

☐ Not applicable.

☐ Not enough information.

Q46 Comments:

Q47 Assessment/feedback

[Who develops and manages the assessment (instructor, provider via software), structure, and whether it is individualized to student learning and relevant to stated learning goals; data accessible to users]

☐ [4] Student learning is assessed frequently in varied formats that facilitate learning opportunities.

☐ [3] Student learning is assessed frequently in a single format that facilitates learning.

☐ [2] Student learning is assessed once in a way that facilitates learning opportunities.

☐ [1] Student learning is assessed during the session but is not constructive towards learning.

☐ [0] Student learning is not assessed during the session.

☐ Not applicable.

☐ Not enough information.

Q48 Comments:

Q40 Narrative Vignette:

Q50 Miscellaneous notes:

B

Classroom Walk-Through Instrument

Purpose:

- Collect basic descriptive data on the implementation of digital instructional tools in schools (NOT to gauge engagement or quality of instructional session)
- Develop a "profile" of implementation for various digital instructional tools, ideally at the school level
- Aligned to the existing walk-through procedures, including the "Organizing Physical Space domain in the Danielson Framework"

Process:

- Filled out by observer during a walk of instructional sessions
- Duration of 10–15 minutes per walk

Observer name/role: _____ / _____

Date:	Time: _____ – _____ Block: Y N	School:
Grade band: K–2 3–5 6–8 9–12	Number of staff present:	Number of students present:
Instruction	Session type • Core classroom • Intervention classroom • Credit recovery • Study hall • Out of school time • Other _____ Facility • Computer lab • Classroom • Library • Home • Other _____ Content • Math • Language arts • Social Studies • Science • Technology • Arts • Other _____	
Digital Tools Students/device: ____/____ P=present, U=in use I=instructor, S=student	Hardware [present/in-use][instructor/student]: • Desktop [P/U][I/S] • Laptop [P/U][I/S] • Tablet [P/U][I/S] • Smart phone [P/U][I/S] • Headphone [P/U][I/S] • Smart Board [P/U][I/S] • Yondr/cell phone pouches [P/U][I/S] • Other _____ [P/U][I/S] Software: • Vendor/tool name [P/U][I/S] • Vendor/tool name [P/U][I/S] • LAN School [P/U][I/S] • Khan Academy [P/U][I/S] • Compass [P/U][I/S] • Open Ed [P/U][I/S] • Google Drive [P/U][I/S] • Internet [P/U][I/S] • Other _____ [P/U][I/S]	

Were digital tools functional? Yes No	Describe:
Particular classroom-based strategies being deployed to support the effective use of digital tools? Yes No	Describe:
Brief, 3–4 sentence description of instructional setting and activities:	
Other comments:	

C

Cultural Relevance and Responsiveness Instrument

Rate each item, where *"Rarely"* indicates the item occurred once or twice during the module and *"Often"* indicates that the item occurred regularly during the module. An N/A option is only provided in the assessment strategies sections, as an N/A rating of curricular content and instructional tasks suggest that there are neutral content and tasks. Ratings should be made with that knowledge that choices are always made (i.e., defaulting to the norm is in and of itself a choice). Refer to the attached glossary for definitions and examples of select terms.

When rating curricular content, consider information transmitted through skill introduction, assessments, and other assignments.

Curricular content	Never	Rarely	Sometimes	Often
The module uses content examples from multiple cultural backgrounds (e.g., literature, history, images).	1	2	3	4
The module teaches students about contributions by individuals or societies that belong to minoritized groups.	1	2	3	4
The module explains new concepts using examples that are taken from a diverse representation of everyday life (e.g., financial, political, social).	1	2	3	4
The module provides opportunities for students to use prior knowledge to help them make sense of new information (e.g., by scaffolding new content on prior experiences).	1	2	3	4
The module provides students with the academic knowledge and skills needed to function in the culture of power. (Simply teaching within that framework is insufficient to prepare students.)	1	2	3	4
The culture of power is made explicit.	1	2	3	4
The module counters the dominant narrative of white male authority and power (e.g., shows women or minoritized populations in positions of power).	1	2	3	4
The module acknowledges current sociopolitical realities (of minoritized and/or dominant groups) versus essentializing a culture or group of people.	1	2	3	4

Instructional tasks	Never	Rarely	Sometimes	Often
The module uses a variety of teaching methods (e.g., visual and auditory elements of a lecture, guided practice, student-directed investigation) to help meet the needs of all students.	1	2	3	4
The module uses the interests of students to make the learning process meaningful for them (e.g., choice involved in generating an open-ended response).	1	2	3	4
The module prioritizes depth over breadth by engaging students in increasingly complex activities around a particular topic or learning goal (e.g., requires analysis, synthesis, or application).	1	2	3	4
The module incorporates tasks that require students to apply their learning to an issue, context, or problem beyond school.	1	2	3	4

Below, select N/A only if the module never assessed student learning.

Assessment strategies	Never	Rarely	Sometimes	Often	N/A
The module assesses student learning using various types of assessments, such as self-assessment and portfolios, to evaluate students' performance.	1	2	3	4	N/A
The module assesses students' readiness, strengths and weaknesses, and development needs.	1	2	3	4	N/A
The module integrates assessment items or strategies that considers and incorporates linguistically or culturally diverse content.	1	2	3	4	N/A
The module integrates assessment items or strategies that adapt to students' level of understanding.	1	2	3	4	N/A

Provide a detailed description of the module to expand on the above items, including but not limited to:

- Content
- Instructional tasks
- Assessments
- Implicit (or explicit) values, expectations, norms, or beliefs expressed by the instructor or course content.

Glossary

Beliefs: Something one accepts as true or real; a firmly held opinion or conviction (e.g., that capitalism meets consumers' needs by encouraging competition and providing choice).

Culture: The customary beliefs, social forms, and material traits of a racial, religious, or social group (e.g., Chinese, Hispanic, Muslim, Southern); a given individual may belong to various cultures based on intersecting identities.

Culture of power: The ideas, attitudes, or activities that are regarded as normal or conventional, often aligned with dominant culture norms and practices.

Minoritized culture: Cultural beliefs, social forms, and material traits not practiced by the elite political, social, or economic entity that sets social norms. It achieves dominance by being perceived as pertaining to a majority of the population and having a significant presence in institutions relating to communication, education, artistic expression, law, government, and business. In the United States, this term is often used in contrast to white, middle-/upper-class, heteronormative, Christian norms and practices.

Norms: A standard or pattern, especially of social behavior, that is typical or expected of a group (e.g., in white, middle-class, American corporate culture, you are expected to greet someone by shaking hands).

Sociopolitical: Involving both social and political factors (e.g., social safety net programs are influenced both by social perceptions and stigma surrounding public aid as well as related governmental policy and program administration).

Values: Principles or standards of behavior; one's judgment of what is important in life (e.g., individualism, material success, and democracy within white, middle-class, American culture).

APPENDIX

D

Authentic Online Work Rubric

Complete the following rubric for each lesson observed.

Lesson Information

Which of the following components are included in the lesson?

☐ Warm-up
☐ Lecture
☐ Practice
☐ Assessment
☐ Writing
☐ Interactive (e.g., lab, performance)
☐ Other (please describe)

Total number of minutes required to watch the lecture videos (round to the nearest minute): ___

Number of minutes spent related to particular instructional expectations. (You may allocate the same minute to more than one instructional expectation. The total number of minutes will likely exceed the total lecture length.):

____ Skill introduction
____ Drilling/practice

____ Review

____ Assessment

____ Games

____ Enrichment/accelerated instruction

____ Other (please describe)

Which of the following orders of thinking are required to complete instructional tasks?

☐ Listen

☐ Recite/remember

☐ Demonstrate

☐ Think critically

☐ Apply

☐ Synthesize

☐ Evaluate

☐ Create

Higher-Order Thinking

Rate each item, where "Rarely" indicates the item occurred once or twice during the lesson and "Often" indicates that the item occurred all but once or twice during the lesson.

	Never	Rarely	Sometimes	Often
Students spent instructional time generating knowledge (versus direct instruction).	1	2	3	4
Assessment questions, practice problems, and other instructional tasks were delivered in an open-response format (i.e., not multiple choice or true/false).	1	2	3	4
Assessment questions, practice problems, and other instructional tasks allow for various correct responses (i.e., open-response questions that allow students to apply concepts to a topic of their choosing).	1	2	3	4
There was more than one method for generating an acceptable response.	1	2	3	4
Assignments required students to gather information on their own.	1	2	3	4
Students were asked challenging questions and/or to perform challenging tasks (such as those requiring extensive prior content knowledge, multiple steps, or the application of multiple concepts.)	1	2	3	4
Students were asked to offer reasoning to support responses.	1	2	3	4

Real-World Relevance

Rate each item, where "Rarely" indicates the item occurred once or twice during the lesson and "Often" indicates that the item occurred all but once or twice during the lesson.

	Never	Rarely	Sometimes	Often
Assessment or instructional tasks were embedding in a specific, meaningful context.	1	2	3	4
Assessment or instructional tasks asked students to synthesize, interpret, explain, or evaluate complex information in addressing a concept, problem, or issue.	1	2	3	4
Students were asked to create work product that had value in its own right outside of the school setting.	1	2	3	4
Assessment or instructional tasks asked students to elaborate their understanding, explanations, or conclusions through extended writing.	1	2	3	4

Describe and include personal reflections on the content, skill focus, and instructional tasks included in this lesson. Also describe any implicit (or explicit) values, expectations, norms, or beliefs expressed by the instructor or course content.

Notes

Introduction

1. The definition of digital learning is from Patricia Burch, Annalee Good, and Carolyn J. Heinrich, "Improving Access to, Quality and the Effectiveness of Digital Instruction in K–12 Education," *Educational Evaluation and Policy Analysis* 38, no. 1 (2016): 65–87.
2. John Wells and Laurie Lewis, "Internet Access in U.S. Public Schools and Classrooms: 1994–2005," NCES 2007-020 (Washington, DC: US Department of Education, National Center for Education Statistics, 2006).
3. Gloria Ladson-Billings, "From the Achievement Gap to the Education Debt: Understanding Achievement in US Schools," *Educational Researcher* 35, no. 7 (2006): 3–12.
4. Mark Warschauer, *Learning in the Cloud: How (and Why) to Transform Schools with Digital Media* (New York: Teachers College Press, 2011).
5. S. Craig Watkins, *The Digital Edge: How Black and Latino Youth Navigate Digital Inequality* (New York: New York University Press, 2018).
6. EducationSuperHighway, *2019 State of the States Report*, https://stateofthestates .educationsuperhighway.org/?utm_source=release&utm_medium=newsroom& utm_campaign=SotS18#national.
7. We define *low-resource* as contexts where schools may lack sufficient funds to meet basic operating and educational costs that support access to physical infrastructure, technical capacity, and human capital.
8. WalletHub assessed the gaps between blacks and whites using data on twenty-two key indicators of equality and integration in the fifty states and District of Columbia, including measures of median annual income and standardized test scores; see https://wallethub.com/edu/states-with-the-most-and-least-racial -progress/18428/.
9. Patricia Burch and Annalee Good, *Equal Scrutiny: Privatization and Accountability in Digital Education* (Cambridge, MA: Harvard Education Press, 2014). The FCC's E-Rate program makes telecommunications and information services more affordable for schools and libraries. With funding from the Universal Service Fund (fcc.gov/encyclopedia/universal-service-fund), E-Rate provides discounts for telecommunications, internet access, and internal connections to eligible schools and libraries (from https://www.fcc.gov/consumers/guides/universal-service -program-schools-and-libraries-e-rate).
10. Barbara Means et al., *Evaluation of Evidence-Based Practices in Online Learning: A Meta-analysis and Review of Online Learning Studies* (Washington, DC: US Department of Education, 2010).

11. In 2013, the Los Angeles Unified School District initiated a $1.3 billion program to provide every student with a tablet computer and digital curricula to propel digital instruction, but the program—plagued by insufficient training, faulty software, and massive cost overruns on an already strained budget, not to mention questionable bidding practices—collapsed within two years. Tod Newcombe, "A Cautionary Tale for Any Government IT Project: L.A.'s Failed iPad Program," *Governing*, 2015, http://www.governing.com/columns/tech-talk/gov-tablets-los -angeles-ipad-apple-schools.html.

12. Richard Milner, *Rac(e)ing to Class: Confronting Poverty and Race in Schools and Classrooms* (Cambridge, MA: Harvard Education Press, 2015), 34.

13. Thurston Domina, Andrew Penner, and Emily Penner, "Categorical Inequality: Schools as Sorting Machines," *Annual Review of Sociology* 43 (2017): 311–330.

14. Harry Brighouse et al., *Educational Goods: Values, Evidence, and Decision-Making* (Chicago: University of Chicago Press, 2018).

15. Noel Enyedy, *Personalized Instruction: New Interest, Old Rhetoric, Limited Results, and the Need for a New Direction for Computer-Mediated Learning* (Boulder, CO: National Education Policy Center, 2014); Binbin Zheng et al., "Learning in One-to-One Laptop Environments: A Meta-Analysis and Research Synthesis," *Review of Educational Research* 86, no. 4 (2016): 1052–1084.

16. Adolph. J. Delgado et al., "Educational Technology: A Review of the Integration, Resources, and Effectiveness of Technology in K–12 Classrooms," *Journal of Information Technology Education: Research* 14 (2015): 397–416.

17. Tina N. Hohlfeld et al., "An Examination of Seven Years of Technology Integration in Florida Schools: Through the Lens of the Levels of Digital Divide in Schools," *Computers & Education* 113 (2017): 135–161.

18. Mark Warschauer and Tina Matuchniak, "New Technology and Digital Worlds: Analyzing Evidence of Equity in Access, Use, and Outcomes," *Review of Research in Education* 34 (2010): 179–225.

19. David Stevens et al., *Online Credit Recovery: Enrollment and Passing Patterns in Montana Digital Academy Courses* (Washington, DC: US Department of Education, Institute of Education Sciences, National Center for Education Evaluation and Regional Assistance, Regional Educational Laboratory Northwest, 2016).

20. Wayne Au, *Critical Curriculum Studies: Education, Consciousness, and the Politics of Knowing* (London: Routledge, 2012).

21. Burch and Good, *Equal Scrutiny.*

22. H. M. Marks, "Student Engagement in Instructional Activity: Patterns in the Elementary, Middle, and High School Years," *American Educational Research Journal* 37, no. 1 (2000): 153–184.

23. Marks, "Student Engagement in Instructional Activity"; and F. Newmann, G. G Wehlage, and S. D. Lamborn, "The Significance and Sources of Student Engagement," in *Student Engagement and Achievement in American Secondary Schools*, ed. F. Newmann (New York: Teachers College Press, 1992), 11–39.

24. J. Darling-Aduana, "Authenticity, Engagement, and Performance in Online High School Courses: Insights from Micro-interactional Data" (working paper, Georgia State University, College of Education and Human Development, Learning Sciences, 2020).

Chapter 1

1. https://scholars.org/brief/what-state-and-local-agencies-need-know-making-large-scale-purchases-digital-technologies.
2. http://www.jivdayafound.org/step-program-overview.
3. Carolyn J. Heinrich and Annalee Good, "Research-Informed Practice Improvements: Exploring Linkages Between School District Use of Research Evidence and Educational Outcomes over Time," *School Effectiveness and School Improvement* 29, no. 3 (2018): 418–445.
4. Mauro F. Guillén and Sandra L. Suárez, "Explaining the Global Digital Divide: Economic, Political and Sociological Drivers of Cross-National Internet Use," *Social Forces* 84, no. 2 (2005): 681–708, http://www.jstor.org.ezproxy.lib.utexas.edu/stable/3598474.
5. Guillén and Suárez, "Explaining the Global Digital Divide."
6. Noel Enyedy, *Personalized Instruction: New Interest, Old Rhetoric, Limited Results, and the Need for a New Direction for Computer-Mediated Learning* (Boulder, CO: National Education Policy Center, 2014). Retrieved on November 26, 2014, from http://nepc.colorado.edu/publication/personalized-instruction.
7. John Wells and Laurie Lewis, *Internet Access in US Public Schools and Classrooms: 1994–2005*, NCES 2007-020 (Washington, DC: US Department of Education, National Center for Education Statistics, 2000).
8. Audrey Watters, "The History of the Future of E-Rate and Affordable Internet Access at Schools," *Hack Education*, March 8, 2017, http://hackeducation.com/2017/03/08/history-of-e-rate.
9. https://cbcommunity.comcast.com/browse-all/details/digital-transformation-2.0-the-next-phase-for-education.
10. See NCLB Public Law 107–110–8, January 2002, and Brian Rowan, "The New Institutionalism and the Study of Educational Organizations: Changing Ideas for Changing Times," in *The New Institutionalism in Education*, ed. Hans-Dieter Meyer and Brian Rowan (Albany: State University of New York Press, 2006), 15–32.
11. Patricia Burch, *Hidden Markets: The New Education Privatization* (New York: Routledge, 2009); Patricia Burch, Annalee Good, and Carolyn J. Heinrich, "Improving Access to Quality and the Effectiveness of Digital Instruction in K–12 Education," *Educational Evaluation and Policy Analysis* 38, no. 1 (2016): 65–87.
12. Patricia Burch and Annalee G. Good, *Equal Scrutiny: Privatization and Accountability in Digital Education* (Cambridge, MA: Harvard Education Press, 2014), 14.
13. Kelsey Sheehy, "States, Districts Require Online Ed for High School Graduation," *US News & World Report*, October 24, 2012.
14. Anique Scheerder, Alexander J. A. M. Van Deursen, and Jan A. G. M..Van Dijk, "Determinants of Internet Skills, Uses and Outcomes: A Systematic Review of the Second- and Third-Level Digital Divide," *Telematics and Informatics* 34, no. 8 (2017): 1607–1624, doi:10.1016/j.tele.2017.07.007.
15. Betheny Gross, Sivan Tuchman, and Susan Patrick, *A National Landscape Scan of Personalized Learning in K–12 Education in the United States* (Vienna, VA: iNACOL, 2018), 4.

16. Enyedy, *Personalized Instruction.*
17. Gross, Tuchman, and Patrick, *A National Landscape Scan.*
18. Elizabeth D. Steiner et al., *Designing Innovative High Schools*, RR-2005-CCNY (Santa Monica, CA: RAND Corporation, 2017).
19. Benjamin Herold, "Personalized Learning: Modest Gains, Big Challenges, RAND Study Finds," *Education Week*, July 11, 2017.
20. Gross, Tuchman, and Patrick, *A National Landscape Scan*, 6.
21. Steiner et al., *Designing Innovative High Schools.*
22. https://www.insidehighered.com/digital-learning/blogs/technology-and-learning /technology-driving-educational-inequality.
23. Richard Milner, *Rac(e)ing to Class: Confronting Poverty and Race in Schools and Classrooms* (Cambridge, MA: Harvard Education Press, 2015), 33, 46–47.
24. Gretchen Brion-Meisels. "'Can I Trust You With This?' Investigating Middle School Students' Use Of Learning Supports," *Urban Education* 50, no. 6 (2015): 718–749; Gretchen Brion-Meisels, "'It Starts Out with Little Things': An Exploration of Urban Adolescents' Support-Seeking Strategies in the Context of School," *Teachers College Record* 118, no.1 (2016): 1–38; Milner, *Rac(e)ing to Class*, 33.

Chapter 2

1. The Future Ready Framework is a structure for digital learning visioning, planning, and implementation focused on student-centered learning designed by the Alliance for Excellent education; more details are available at https://futureready .org/about-the-effort/framework/.
2. More information on the Wisconsin Digital Learning Plan and the WDLC is available at www.dpi.wi.gov/digital-learning.
3. Patrick Thomas and Erin Richards, "Online Schools and Student Mobility: When Kids Churn, Scores Drop," *Milwaukee Journal Sentinel*, November 5, 2018, https://projects.jsonline.com/news/2018/11/5/online-schools-popular-but-40 -percent-students-dont-stay.html.
4. For more details on the Classroom Connectivity Initiative, see https://tea.texas .gov/Classroom_Connectivity/.
5. TEC, §30A.007.
6. Patricia Burch and Annalee Good, *Equal Scrutiny: Privatization and Accountability in Digital Education* (Cambridge, MA: Harvard Education Press, 2014).

Chapter 3

1. Theodore J. Kopcha, "Teachers' Perceptions of the Barriers to Technology Integration and Practices with Technology Under Situated Professional Development," *Computers & Education* 59, no. 4 (2012): 1109–1121; Jo Tondeur et al., "Preparing Pre-Service Teachers to Integrate Technology in Education: A Synthesis of Qualitative Evidence," *Computers & Education* 59, no. 1 (2012): 134–144.
2. Susan Patrick, Kathryn Kennedy, and Allison Powell, *Mean What You Say: Defining and Integrating Personalized, Blended and Competency Education* (Vienna, VA: iNACOL, 2013), https://www.inacol.org/wp-content/uploads/2015/02/mean -what-you-say-1.pdf.
3. Barbara Means et al., *Evaluation of Evidence-Based Practices in Online Learning: A Meta-Analysis and Review of Online Learning Studies* (Washington, DC:

US Department of Education, 2009); Yong Zhao et al., "What Makes the Difference? A Practical Analysis of Research on the Effectiveness of Distance Education," *Teachers College Record* 107, no. 8 (2005): 1836–1884.

4. Russell W. Rumberger and Sun Ah Lim, "Why Students Drop Out of School: A Review of 25 Years of Research," *California Dropout Research Project* 15 (2008): 1–3.

5. Gretchen Brion-Meisels, "'Can I Trust You with This?' Investigating Middle School Students' Use of Learning Supports," *Urban Education* 50, no. 6 (2015): 718–749; Gretchen Brion-Meisels, "'It Starts Out with Little Things': An Exploration of Urban Adolescents' Support-Seeking Strategies in the Context of School," *Teachers College Record* 118, no. 1 (2016): 1–38.

6. June Ahn, "Policy, Technology, and Practice in Cyber Charter Schools: Framing the Issues," *Teachers College Record* 113, no. 1 (2011): 1–26.

7. David Furió et al., "Mobile Learning vs. Traditional Classroom Lessons: A Comparative Study," *Journal of Computer Assisted Learning* 31, no. 3 (2015): 189–201; Neil Selwyn, *Is Technology Good for Education?* (Cambridge: United Kingdom Polity Press, 2016).

8. Jennifer Darling-Aduana, Annalee Good, and Carolyn J. Heinrich, "Mapping the Inequity Implications of Help-Seeking in Online Credit-Recovery Classrooms," *Teachers College Record* 121, no. 11 (2019): 1–40.

9. Tondeur et al., "Preparing Pre-Service Teachers to Integrate Technology in Education."

10. Tina N. Hohlfeld et al., "An Examination of Seven Years of Technology Integration in Florida Schools: Through the Lens of the Levels of Digital Divide in Schools," *Computers & Education* 113 (2017): 135–161; Mark Warschauer, *Laptops and Literacy: Learning in the Wireless Classroom* (New York: Teachers College Press, 2006).

11. Bjoern Haßler, Louis Major, and Sara Hennessy, "Tablet Use in Schools: A Critical Review of the Evidence for Learning Outcomes," *Journal of Computer Assisted Learning* 32, no. 2 (2016): 139–156.

12. Ferry Boschman et al., "Exploring the Role of Content Knowledge in Teacher Design Conversations," *Journal of Computer Assisted Learning* 32, no. 2 (2016): 157–169.

13. Courtney K. Blackwell, Alexis R. Lauricella, and Ellen Wartella, "The Influence of TPACK Contextual Factors on Early Childhood Educators' Tablet Computer Use," *Computers & Education* 98 (2016): 57–69; Larry Cuban, *Oversold and Underused: Computers in the Classroom* (Cambridge, MA: Harvard University Press, 2009); Daniel S. Stanhope and Jennifer O. Corn, "Acquiring Teacher Commitment to 1:1 Initiatives: The Role of the Technology Facilitator," *Journal of Research on Technology in Education* 46, no. 3 (2014): 252–276.

14. Laura M. Desimone, "Improving Impact Studies of Teachers' Professional Development: Toward Better Conceptualizations and Measures," *Educational Researcher* 38, no. 3 (2009): 181–199; Fethi A. Inan and Deborah L. Lowther, "Laptops in the K–12 Classrooms: Exploring Factors Impacting Instructional Use," *Computers & Education* 55, no. 3 (2010): 937–944; Kopcha, "Teachers' Perceptions of the Barriers to Technology Integration."

15. Thomas R. Guskey, "Professional Development and Teacher Change," *Teachers and Teaching* 8, no. 3 (2002): 381–391; V. Darleen Opfer and David Pedder,

"Conceptualizing Teacher Professional Learning," *Review of Educational Research* 81, no. 3 (2011): 376–407.

16. Richard L. Venezky, "Technology in the Classroom: Steps Toward a New Vision," *Education, Communication & Information* 4, no. 1 (2004): 3–21.

17. Selwyn, *Is Technology Good for Education?*

18. Jessica B. Heppen et al., "The Struggle to Pass Algebra: Online vs. Face-To-Face Credit Recovery for At-Risk Urban Students," *Journal of Research on Educational Effectiveness* 10, no. 2 (2017): 272–296.

19. Patricia A. DiCerbo et al., "A Review of the Literature on Teaching Academic English to English Language Learners," *Review of Educational Research* 84, no. 3 (2014): 446–482.

20. George C. Bunch, "Pedagogical Language Knowledge: Preparing Mainstream Teachers for English Learners in the New Standards Era," *Review of Research in Education* 37, no. 1 (2013): 298–341; DiCerbo et al., "A Review of the Literature."

21. Melinda R. Snodgrass, Maya Israel, and George C. Reese, "Instructional Supports for Students with Disabilities in K–5 Computing: Findings from a Cross-Case Analysis," *Computers & Education* 100 (2016): 1–17.

22. Selwyn, *Is Technology Good for Education?*

23. Jennifer Darling-Aduana, "Behavioral Engagement Shifts Among At-Risk High School Students Enrolled in Online Course," *AERA Open* (2019); Rumberger and Lim. "Why Students Drop Out of School."

24. Cynthia S. Bambara et al., "Delicate Engagement: The Lived Experience of Community College Students Enrolled in High-Risk Online Courses," *Community College Review* 36, no. 3 (2009): 219–238; Shanna Smith Jaggars, "Choosing Between Online and Face-to-Face Courses: Community College Student Voices," *American Journal of Distance Education* 28, no. 1 (2014): 27–38; Di Xu and Shanna S. Jaggars, "Performance Gaps Between Online and Face-to-Face Courses: Differences Across Types of Students and Academic Subject Areas," *Journal of Higher Education* 85, no. 5 (2014): 633–659.

Chapter 4

1. Anique Scheerder, Alexander J. A. M. Van Deursen, and Jan A. G. M. Van Dijk, "Determinants of Internet Skills, Uses and Outcomes: A Systematic Review of the Second- and Third-Level Digital Divide," *Telematics and Informatics* 34, no. 8 (2017): 1607–1624, doi:10.1016/j.tele.2017.07.007.

2. https://marketbrief.edweek.org/marketplace-K–12/districts-used-7000-tech-tools -year-ones-popular/.

3. Scheerder, Van Deursen, and Van Dijk, "Determinants of Internet Skills, Uses and Outcomes."

4. Sumeda Chauhan, "A Meta-Analysis of the Impact of Technology on Learning Effectiveness of Elementary Students," *Computers and Education* 105 (2017): 14–30.

5. Barbara Means et al., *Evaluation of Evidence-Based Practices in Online Learning: A Meta-Analysis and Review of Online Learning Studies* (Washington, DC: US Department of Education Office of Planning, Evaluation, and Policy Development Policy and Program Studies Service, 2010).

6. Patrick, Helen, Allison M. Ryan, and Avi Kaplan. "Early Adolescents' Perceptions of the Classroom Social Environment, Motivational Beliefs, and Engagement," *Journal of Educational Psychology* 99, no. 1 (2007): 83; Ellen A. Skinner, James G. Wellborn, and James P. Connell, "What It Takes to Do Well in School and Whether I've Got It: A Process Model of Perceived Control and Children's Engagement and Achievement in School," *Journal of Educational Psychology* 82, no. 1 (1990): 22; Ming-Te Wang, and Rebecca Holcombe, "Adolescents' Perceptions of School Environment, Engagement, and Academic Achievement in Middle School," *American Educational Research Journal* 47, no. 3 (2010): 633–662.

7. Ellen A. Skinner, Thomas A. Kindermann, and Carrie J. Furrer, "A Motivational Perspective on Engagement and Disaffection: Conceptualization and Assessment of Children's Behavioral and Emotional Participation in Academic Activities in the Classroom," *Educational and Psychological Measurement* 69 *(*2009): 493–525.

8. Jennifer Darling-Aduana and Carolyn J. Heinrich, "The Role of Teacher Capacity and Instructional Practice in the Integration of Educational Technology for Emergent Bilingual Students," *Computers & Education* 126 (2018): 417–432.

9. Allison Powell, Verena Roberts, and Susan Patrick, *Using Online Learning for Credit Recovery: Getting Back on Track to Graduation* (Vienna, VA: *i*NACOL, 2015), http://www.aurora-institute.org/wp-content/uploads/iNACOL_Using OnlineLearningForCreditRecovery.pdf.

10. Brian Thevenot and Sarah Butrymowicz, "Solving the Dropout Problem?" *Texas Tribune* and the Hechinger Report, November 5, 2010.

11. Craig Clough, "Provider of Online Credit Recovery Courses at LAUSD Says Curriculum Is 'Very Rigorous' Despite Criticism," *LA School Report*, September 7, 2016.

12. Susan Patrick, Kathryn Kennedy, and Allison Powell, *Mean What You Say: Defining and Integrating Personalized, Blended and Competency Education* (Vienna, VA: iNACOL, 2013).

13. Wayne Au, *Critical Curriculum Studies: Education, Consciousness, and the Politics of Knowing* (New York: Routledge, 2012).

14. André Brock, "'A Belief in Humanity Is a Belief in Colored Men': Using Culture to Span the Digital Divide," *Journal of Computer-Mediated Communication* 11, no. 1 (2005): 357–374; Anne W. Rawls, "'Race' as an Interaction Order Phenomenon: WEB Du Bois's 'Double Consciousness' Thesis Revisited," *Sociological Theory* 18, no. 2 (2000): 241–274.

15. Elman Yukselturk and Safure Bulut, "Predictors for Student Success in an Online Course," *Journal of Educational Technology and Society* 10, no. 2 (2007): 71–83.

16. Geneva Gay, *Culturally Responsive Teaching: Theory, Research, and Practice* (New York: Teachers College Press, 2010).

17. Gay, *Culturally Responsive Teaching*.

18. Shirley B. Heath, "Questioning at Home and at School: A Comparative Study," in *Doing the Ethnography of Schooling: Educational Anthropology in Action*, ed. George D. Spindler (New York: Holt, Rinehart, and Winston, 1982), 102–131.

19. Tina Barrios et al., *Laptops for Learning: Final Report and Recommendations of the Laptops for Learning Task Force* (Tallahassee: Florida Department of Education, 2004).

20. Eighty-six percent of observations with a substitute teacher received the lowest rat-ings (0 or 1) on instructor engagement, compared with 38 percent of observations without a substitute.

Chapter 5

1. NCLB is described as "An act to close the achievement gap with accountability, flexibility, and choice, so that no child is left behind" (Public Law 107-110 [Wash-ington, DC: US Government Publishing Office, January 8, 2002]), https://www .govinfo.gov/link/plaw/107/public/110?link-type=pdf.
2. US Department of Education, *2015 National Assessment of Educational Progress* (Washington, DC: Institute of Education Sciences, NAEP, 2015).
3. US Department of Education, *State Nonfiscal Survey of Public Elementary and Secondary Education, 2008–09 through 2014–15* (Washington, DC: Institute of Education Sciences, 2016).
4. Jennifer Darling-Aduana and Carolyn J. Heinrich, "The Role of Teacher Capacity and Instructional Practice in the Integration of Educational Technology for Emer-gent Bilingual Students," *Computers & Education* 126 (2018): 417–432.
5. George C. Bunch, "Pedagogical Language Knowledge: Preparing Mainstream Teachers for English Learners in the New Standards Era," *Review of Research in Education* 37, no.1 (2013): 298–341; Patricia A. DiCerbo et al., "A Review of the Literature on Teaching Academic English to English Language Learners," *Review of Research in Education* 84, no. 3 (2014): 446–482.
6. Carolyn J. Heinrich et al., "A Look Inside Online Educational Settings in High School: Promise and Pitfalls for Improving Educational Opportunities and Out-comes." *American Educational Research Journal* 56, no. 6 (2019): 2147–2188.
7. "The Rise in American High-School Graduation Rates Looks Puffed-Up," *The Economist*, January 3, 2019. The NAEP is the largest ongoing nationally repre-sentative assessment of student math and reading achievement; see https://nces .ed.gov/nationsreportcard/.
8. See https://nces.ed.gov/fastfacts/display.asp?id=51.
9. Carolyn J. Heinrich and Jennifer Darling-Aduana, "Does Online Course-Taking Increase High School Completion and Open Pathways to Postsecondary Education Opportunities?" (working paper, Vanderbilt University, 2019).
10. Allison Powell, Susan Patrick, and Verena Roberts, *Using Online Learning for Credit Recovery: Getting Back on Track to Graduation* (Vienna, VA: iNACOL, 2015), https://www.inacol.org/wp-content/uploads/2015/09/iNACOL_Using OnlineLearningForCreditRecovery.pdf, p. 10.
11. Carolyn J. Heinrich and Annalee Good, "Research-Informed Practice Improve-ments: Exploring Linkages Between School District Use of Research Evidence and Educational Outcomes over Time," *School Effectiveness and School Improvement* 29, no. 3 (2018): 418–445.

Chapter 6

1. Elizabeth D. Steiner et al., *Designing Innovative High Schools*, RR-2005-CCNY (Santa Monica, CA: RAND Corporation, 2017).
2. US Department of Education, Office of Educational Technology letter, 2017, https://tech.ed.gov/funding/.

3. Jennifer Darling-Aduana, Annalee Good, and Carolyn J. Heinrich, "Mapping the Inequity Implications of Help-Seeking in Online Credit-Recovery Classrooms," *Teachers College Record* 121, no. 11 (2019).

4. Fabienne Doucet and Jennifer Adair, "Addressing Race and Inequity in the Classroom," *Young Children* 68, no. 5 (2013): 88–97.

5. "We Asked About School Finance. What Did Districts Say?" *Education Week*, September 25, 2019, https://www.edweek.org/ew/articles/2019/09/25/we-asked -about-school-finance-what-did.html.

6. Patricia E. Holland, "Professional Development in Technology: Catalyst for School Reform," *Journal of Technology and Teacher Education* 9, no. 2 (2001): 245–267.

7. Larry Cuban, *Inside the Black Box of Classroom Practice: Change Without Reform in American Education* (Cambridge, MA: Harvard Education Press, 2013); Benjamin Herold, "Why Ed Tech Is Not Transforming How Teachers Teach," *Education Week*, June 10, 2015, https://www.edweek.org/ew/articles/2015/06/11 /why-ed-tech-is-not-transforming-how.html; Kelly Shapley et al., *Evaluation of the Texas Technology Immersion Pilot: Final Outcomes for a Four-Year Study (2004–05 to 2007–08)* (Austin: Texas Center for Educational Research, 2009).

8. Wayne Au, *Critical Curriculum Studies: Education, Consciousness, and the Politics of Knowing* (New York: Routledge, 2012); Thomas Dee and Emily Penner, "The Causal Effects of Cultural Relevance: Evidence from an Ethnic Studies Curriculum," *American Educational Research Journal* 54, no. 1 (2017): 127–166; Thomas Dee and Emily Penner, *My Brother's Keeper? The Impact of Targeted Educational Supports* (CEPA Working Paper No.19-07, 2019), http://cepa.stanford .edu/wp19-07.

9. Lisa Delpit, *Other People's Children: Cultural Conflict in the Curriculum* (New York: The New Press, 1995).

10. Elizabeth City et al., *Instructional Rounds in Education: A Networked Approach to Improving Teaching and Learning* (Cambridge, MA: Harvard Education Press, 2009).

Acknowledgments

We thank Jaime and Pilar Davila and the William T. Grant Foundation for generous funding of this research. We also thank Dr. Vinay Jain, the founder of the Jiv Daya Foundation, and his staff, particularly Tina Chong, the Education Program Manager, for their collaboration and contributions to this project in Dallas. We greatly appreciate the partnership and opportunity to learn with our school district partners, the Dallas Independent School District and Milwaukee Public Schools, and all of the administrators, staff members, and teachers who opened the doors to their learning spaces and engaged in discussions throughout the project. We especially thank Roland Antoine of Dallas and Sandy Schroeder, Kristin Kappelman, William Luedtke, John Hill, and Marc Sanders of Milwaukee for their long-term engagement with this project. We are grateful as well to the technology vendors that facilitated access to data from online instructional systems used in Milwaukee. And lastly, but perhaps most importantly, we are also thankful for the valuable research support provided by our many research assistants over the course of this project, including: Huiping (Emily) Cheng, Elisabeth Geraghty, Kathy Villalon, and Ja'Dell Davis of the University of Wisconsin-Madison; Esmeralda Garcia Galvan, Christi Kirshbaum, Matt Farber, and Chandi Wagner (formerly of the University of Texas at Austin); Christopher J. (CJ) Ryan, Mason Shero, Jacqueline Aboulafia, and Hillary Bendert in their time at Vanderbilt University, and to other staff at the University of Wisconsin-Madison, Vanderbilt University, and University of Texas at Austin for administrative support of this initiative.

About the Authors

Carolyn J. Heinrich is the Patricia and Rodes Hart Professor of Public Policy and Education and Chair of the Department of Leadership, Policy, and Organizations, and an affiliated Professor of Economics at Vanderbilt University. Her research focuses on education, workforce development, social welfare policy and poverty reduction, program evaluation, and public management and performance management issues. She conducts research in both US and international contexts and often works closely with federal, state, and local governments and nongovernmental organizations to improve policy and program design and effectiveness. In 2004, she received the David N. Kershaw Award for distinguished contributions to the field of public policy analysis and management. She is a past president of the Association for Public Policy Analysis and Management (APPAM) and the Public Management Research Association and was elected to the National Academy of Public Administration in 2010.

Jennifer Darling-Aduana is an Assistant Professor of Learning Technologies in the Department of Learning Sciences, College of Education and Human Development, at Georgia State University. She holds a PhD in Education Leadership and Policy Studies from Vanderbilt University. Her research focuses on the equity implications of K–12 educational policies and practices, such as the widespread expansion of digital learning, as well as the more micro student-teacher and student-curriculum interactions that inadvertently contribute to social reproduction in the classroom. She received the AERA Dissertation Grant for her dissertation, "High School Student Experiences and Outcomes in Online Courses."

Annalee G. Good is co-director of the Wisconsin Evaluation Collaborative and Director of the Clinical Program at the Wisconsin Center for Education Research at the University of Wisconsin-Madison. She holds a PhD in Educational Policy Studies from the University of Wisconsin-Madison. In addition to ongoing research on the integration of digital tools in K–12 classrooms, she supports youth-serving organizations through facilitating culturally responsive evaluation, policy engagement, and youth voice in research and evaluation.

Index